CORE SKILLS

Spelling

ISBN-13: 978-1-4190-3408-4

©2008 Harcourt Achieve Inc.

All rights reserved. This book is intended for classroom use and is not for resale or distribution. Each blackline master in this book may be reproduced, with the copyright notice, without permission from the Publisher. Reproduction for an entire school or district is prohibited. No other part of this publication may be reproduced or transmitted in any form or by any means, electronic or mechanical, including photocopying, recording, taping, or any information storage and retrieval system, without permission in writing from the Publisher.
Contact: Paralegal Department, 6277 Sea Harbor Drive, Orlando, FL 32887.

Steck-Vaughn is a trademark of Harcourt Achieve Inc.

The paper used in this book comes from sustainable resources.

Printed in the United States of America.
6 7 8 9   1413   13 12
4500347973

Steck Vaughn
A Harcourt Achieve Imprint

www.HarcourtSchoolSupply.com
1-800-531-5015

Contents

www.harcourtschoolsupply.com
© Harcourt Achieve Inc. All rights reserved.

Contents
Core Skills Spelling 4, SV 9781419034084

Introduction

Core Skills: Spelling is a research-based, systematic spelling program developed to help students master spelling. The program is based on three critical goals for students:

- to learn to spell common spelling patterns and troublesome words
- to learn strategies related to sounds and spelling patterns
- to link spelling and meaning

Each book in the *Core Skills: Spelling* program is composed of 30 skill lessons. The majority of skill lessons in this program focus on spellings of vowel sounds. Other skill lessons focus on word structure and content-area words.

Key features of this book include:

- study steps that focus learning,

- a spelling table that contains common spellings for consonant and vowel sounds,

- lessons that build competency and provide visual reinforcement,

- word study that expands vocabulary and meaning,

- engaging vocabulary and context activities that encourage students to explore word meanings and use words in meaningful contexts, and

- challenge sections that present opportunities to enrich vocabulary and extend spelling skills.

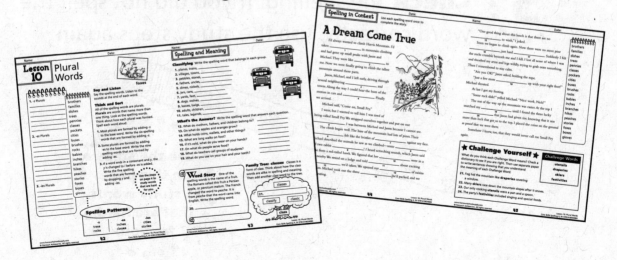

© Harcourt Achieve Inc. All rights reserved.
Core Skills Spelling 4, SV 9781419034084

Study Steps to Learn a Word

 Say the word. What consonant sounds do you hear? What vowel sounds do you hear? How many syllables do you hear?

 Look at the letters in the word. Think about how each sound is spelled. Find any spelling patterns or parts that you know. Close your eyes. Picture the word in your mind.

 Spell the word aloud.

 Write the word. Say each letter as you write it.

 Check the spelling. If you did not spell the word correctly, use the study steps again.

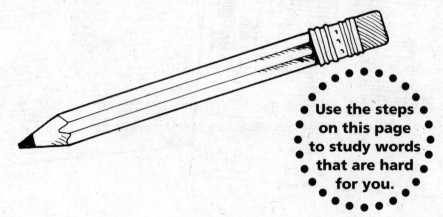

Use the steps on this page to study words that are hard for you.

www.harcourtschoolsupply.com
© Harcourt Achieve Inc. All rights reserved.

Study Steps to Learn a Word
Core Skills Spelling 4, SV 9781419034084

Spelling Table

Sound	Spellings	Examples
/ă/	a ai au	match, plaid, laugh
/ā/	a a_e ai ay ea ei eigh ey	April, chase, plain, day, break, reign, eight, obey
/ä/	a	father
/âr/	air are eir ere ey're	fair, share, their, there, they're
/b/	b bb	bus, rabbit
/ch/	ch tch t	child, match, picture
/d/	d dd	dish, address
/ĕ/	e ea ie ai ue	never, bread, friend, again, guess
/ē/	e e_e ea ee ei eo ey i i_e ie y	zebra, these, please, sweet, deceive, people, key, ski, police, cities, city
/f/	f ff gh	feet, offer, laugh
/g/	g gg	go, jogging
/h/	h wh	hope, who
/ĭ/	i a e ee u ui y	quick, package, secret, been, busy, building, gym
/ī/	i i_e ie igh eye uy y	child, life, die, night, eyesight, buy, dry
/îr/	er ear eer eir ere	period, hear, cheer, weird, here
/j/	j g dg	jog, tragic, edge
/k/	k c ck ch	keep, coast, package, chorus
/ks/	x	axle
/kw/	qu	squeeze
/l/	l ll	life, balloon
/m/	m mb mm	man, comb, swimming

Sound	Spellings	Examples
/n/	n kn nn	nose, knot, beginning
/ng/	n ng	monkey, anything
/ŏ/	o a	doctor, wash
/ō/	o o_e oa oe ow ou ough	zero, those, coach, toe, hollow, boulder, though
/oi/	oi oy	coin, royal
/ô/	o a au augh aw ough	strong, already, cause, taught, shawl, bought
/o͝o/	oo o ou u	wool, wolf, could, full
/o͞o/	oo ew u u_e ue ui o ou	shoot, grew, truly, tune, blue, fruit, two, soup
/ou/	ou ow	ours, towel
/p/	p pp	pay, happen
/r/	r rr wr	reply, hurry, wrinkle
/s/	s ss c	save, pass, fence
/sh/	sh s ce	shape, sugar, ocean
/t/	t tt ed	taste, button, thanked
/th/	th	that
/th/	th	thick
/ŭ/	u o o_e oe oo ou	brush, month, become, does, blood, touch
/ûr/	ur ir er ear ere or our	curve, third, germ, earn, were, world, flourish
/v/	v f	voice, of
/w/	w wh o	win, where, once
/y/	y	yawn
/yo͞o/	u_e ew eau	use, new, beautiful
/z/	z zz s	zebra, blizzard, trees
/ə/	a e i o u	special, often, family, together, surprise

© Harcourt Achieve Inc. All rights reserved.
Core Skills Spelling 4, SV 9781419034084

Lesson 1

Words with Short *a*

stamp

1. *a* Words

_____
_____
_____
_____
_____
_____
_____
_____
_____
_____
_____
_____
_____
_____
_____
_____
_____
_____

2. *au* Words

_____
_____

past
match
ask
snack
stamp
magic
pass
laugh
happen
answer
travel
plastic
grass
aunt
began
crack
glad
branch
half
banana

Say and Listen

Say each spelling word. Listen for the short *a* sound.

Think and Sort

Look at the letters in each word. Think about how short *a* is spelled. Spell each word aloud.

Short *a* can be shown as /ă/. How many spelling patterns for /ă/ do you see?

1. Write the eighteen spelling words that have the *a* pattern.

2. Write the two spelling words that have the *au* pattern.

• Use the steps on page 4 to study words that are hard for you.

Spelling Patterns

a	au
gl**a**d	l**au**gh

Name: _____   Date: _____

Spelling and Meaning

Definitions Write the spelling word for each definition. Use a dictionary if you need to.

1. a sharp snapping sound _____
2. to come to pass _____
3. special effects and tricks _____
4. to go from place to place _____
5. to set a foot down loudly _____
6. green plants that people mow _____
7. a substance made from chemicals _____

Analogies An analogy states that two words go together in the same way as two others. Write the spelling word that completes each analogy.

8. *Opened* is to *closed* as _____ is to *ended*.
9. *Bad* is to *good* as *sad* is to _____.
10. *Three* is to *six* as _____ is to *whole*.
11. *Spin* is to *twirl* as *reply* is to _____.
12. *Large* is to *small* as *feast* is to _____.
13. *Vegetable* is to *spinach* as *fruit* is to _____.
14. *Arm* is to *body* as _____ is to *tree*.
15. *Black* is to *white* as *cry* is to _____.
16. *Male* is to *female* as *uncle* is to _____.
17. *Tomorrow* is to *yesterday* as *future* is to _____.
18. *Question* is to _____ as *tell* is to *answer*.
19. *New* is to *old* as *fail* is to _____.

Word Story Homographs are words that are spelled alike but have different meanings. One spelling word is a homograph that comes from *macche*, meaning "a husband and wife." It also comes from *meiche*, meaning "candlewick." Write the spelling word.

20. _____

Family Tree: *pass* Think about how the *pass* words are alike in spelling and meaning. Then add another *pass* word to the tree.

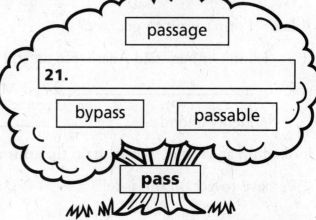

passage

21. _____

bypass   passable

pass

www.harcourtschoolsupply.com
© Harcourt Achieve Inc. All rights reserved.

Lesson 1: Words with Short *a*
Core Skills Spelling 4, SV 9781419034084

Spelling in Context

Use each spelling word once to complete the story.

A Summer Storm

Adam followed his sister down the path from their aunt's cabin. Molly was hurrying to the lake.

"What's taking you so long?" Molly turned to _____ Adam.
                                            1

"I'm trying to catch up," was Adam's _____. He was carrying a bag
                                        2
of apples, a _____, and a big _____ cooler. "I stopped to
                3   4
get a _____ for us to eat."
          5

"We won't have any time to explore the island if we don't hurry," Molly pointed

out. "It's already _____ three."
                        6

They pushed their canoe into the water. As Molly _____ to paddle,
                                                        7
Adam ate an apple. He looked up at the sky. "I don't like the way the clouds look," he

said.

"Oh, they'll _____," Molly told him. "Come on and help me out.
                  8
This isn't a _____ canoe! It won't row by itself. I've paddled
                9
_____ the distance by myself."
        10

Adam reached for a paddle. The canoe tipped dangerously. "Be careful!" Molly told

Adam. "I don't want to get wet."

"I don't either," said Adam. He sat still and carefully began to paddle. Soon he was

able to _____ the speed Molly set. The canoe glided across the lake.
            11
Suddenly a loud _____ of thunder exploded above them. The two
                        12
looked up at the sky. "I was afraid that this might _____!" shouted Adam.
                                                          13
"We have to get off this lake!"

Molly and Adam stopped paddling, wondering if they should _____ on to the island or go back to the cabin. "Back **14** to the cabin!" they shouted at once. Lightning flashed across the sky, and rain began to fall.

Finally they reached the shore. Through the downpour Adam and Molly could see their _____ standing on the cabin **15** porch. She had a worried look on her face. The two children jumped out of the canoe and headed toward her. "Oh, no!" Adam cried as he tripped over a broken tree _____ and fell hard onto **16** the wet green _____. Molly helped him up and they **17** were on their way again. At last they reached the cabin porch.

Adam and Molly began to _____ their feet and **18** shake some of the rain off. "Wow! That was close," Molly said. "I'm _____ we're off that lake!" **19**

Adam nodded and began to _____. "Me too," he **20** said. "We wouldn't want to get wet, now would we?"

Word List
past
match
ask
snack
stamp
magic
pass
laugh
happen
answer
travel
plastic
grass
aunt
began
crack
glad
branch
half
banana

★ Challenge Yourself ★

Challenge Words	
acrobat	axle
absence	tragic

What do you think each Challenge Word means? Check a dictionary to see if you are right. Then use separate paper to write sentences showing that you understand the meaning of each Challenge Word.

21. The **absence** of clouds made us forget that a storm was coming.
22. The road was very bumpy. We thought the wheels on our car would fall off the **axle**.
23. The newspaper reported the **tragic** story of three people lost at sea.
24. The wind made the leaf leap and tumble like a circus **acrobat**.

Name: _____   Date: _____

Lesson 2
Words with Long *a*

chase

1. *a*-consonant-*e* Words

_____
_____
_____
_____
_____
_____
_____
_____
_____
_____

2. *ai* Words

_____
_____
_____
_____
_____
_____

3. *eigh* Words

_____
_____
_____

4. *ea* Word

_____

awake
chase
paid
eight
mistake
plain
trade
weight
waste
afraid
neighbor
taste
trail
plane
wait
waist
space
break
state
shape

Say and Listen
Say each spelling word. Listen for the long *a* sound.

Think and Sort
Look at the letters in each word. Think about how long *a* is spelled. Spell each word aloud.

Long a can be shown as /ā/. How many spelling patterns for /ā/ do you see?

1. Write the ten spelling words that have the *a*-consonant-*e* pattern.

2. Write the six spelling words that have the *ai* pattern.

3. Look at the word *eight*. The spelling pattern for this word is *eigh*. The *g* and *h* are silent. Write the three spelling words that have the *eigh* pattern.

4. Write the one spelling word that has the *ea* pattern.

Use the steps on page 4 to study words that are hard for you.

Spelling Patterns

a-consonant-e	ai	eigh	ea
pl**a**n**e**	p**ai**d	**eigh**t	br**ea**k

www.harcourtschoolsupply.com
© Harcourt Achieve Inc. All rights reserved.

Lesson 2: Words with Long *a*
Core Skills Spelling 4, SV 9781419034084

Spelling and Meaning

Homophones Homophones are words that sound alike but have different spellings and meanings. Complete each sentence with the correct homophone.

1. The present without a ribbon looked very _____.

2. I would rather take a train than a _____.

3. Don't _____ your time looking for the note.

4. Wear the belt around your _____.

5. Alex checked his _____ on the scale.

6. Would you please _____ for me after school?

Rhymes Write the spelling word that completes each sentence and rhymes with the underlined word.

7. I like the _____ of tomato <u>paste</u>.

8. Did the dog _____ the <u>lace</u> ribbon?

9. The boys will _____ the cars they <u>made</u>.

10. Rosa carried a <u>pail</u> down the _____.

11. On what <u>date</u> did Florida become a _____?

12. Draw a <u>face</u> in the empty _____.

13. Ms. <u>Cade</u> _____ for everyone's lunch.

14. What is the _____ of a roll of <u>tape</u>?

15. We have _____ pieces of <u>bait</u> left.

16. Are you ready to <u>take</u> a _____ from your work?

17. It was a _____ to keep the baby <u>awake</u>.

18. He was _____ that he had left the bill <u>unpaid</u>.

19. I want to be _____ when it's time to eat the <u>steak</u>.

Word Story   The Old English word *neahgebur* was made of *neah*, which meant "near," and *gebur*, which meant "dweller." A *neahgebur* was a near dweller. Today the word has the same meaning. Write the word.

20. _____

Family Tree: *break* Think about how the *break* words are alike in spelling and meaning. Then add another *break* word to the tree.

breakfast

21. _____

unbreakable   breaks

break

Name: _____   Date: _____

Spelling in Context

Use each spelling word once to complete the selection.

Safe Places in the Wild

How would you like to have a coyote for a next-door _____ 1 ? Would you be _____ 2 ? When cities grow, people build homes and highways. People and wild animals get closer together. It is _____ 3 that people and wild animals living near one another can lead to problems. The animals do not have _____ 4 to run and hunt. Because letting animals lose their homes would be a big _____ 5 , people make safe places for wild animals. These places are called wildlife refuges.

Many countries, including Canada, Australia, and South Africa, have set aside wildlife refuges. If you live in the United States, your _____ 6 also has one. Special workers are _____ 7 to take care of a refuge. At a large refuge, workers sometimes fly over the area in a _____ 8 . From the air, they check for problems such as flooding or fire. Most refuge workers love their job. They would not _____ 9 it for any other kind.

Visitors do not have to _____ 10 long to see wildlife at a refuge. Picture yourself at a woodland refuge. As you follow a _____ 11 along a creek, seven or _____ 12 deer run past. You see a hungry squirrel _____ 13

open a nut for a snack. You watch a coyote _____ 14 a
mouse through the grass. The mouse does not _____ 15
any time scurrying into a hole! Birds sing and dart from branch to
branch.

   Even at night, the woodland animals are busy. All the raccoons
are _____ 16 and looking for food. They enjoy the sweet
_____ 17 of wild berries. What is that strange, dark
_____ 18 in a tree? It is an owl watching for prey. A
mother opossum slowly waddles past. She carries a lot of
_____ 19 because her babies ride by clinging to her
back. She looks as if she has a belt of babies wrapped around her
_____ 20 !

   Wildlife refuges are special places. The animals have a safe place
to live. People can enjoy them, too. Visitors can take a close look at
animals in the wild.

awake
chase
paid
eight
mistake
plain
trade
weight
waste
afraid
neighbor
taste
trail
plane
wait
waist
space
break
state
shape

★ Challenge Yourself ★

Challenge Words

acquaint
betray
lightweight
reign

Use a dictionary to answer these questions. Then use
separate paper to write sentences showing that
you understand the meaning of each Challenge Word.

21. Can you **acquaint** yourself with people by talking
    to them for a while? _____

22. Would good citizens **betray** their country by selling
    its secrets to an enemy? _____

23. Do dark clouds often come before a **reign**? _____

24. In summer do most people wear **lightweight** clothing? _____

© Harcourt Achieve Inc. All rights reserved.

Lesson 3

Words with Short *e*

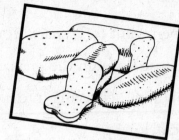

bread

1. *e* Words
_____
_____
_____
_____
_____
_____
_____
_____
_____

2. *ea* Words
_____
_____
_____
_____
_____
_____
_____

3. *ai* Words
_____
_____

4. *ie* Word
_____

5. *ue* Word
_____

again
edge
bread
ever
ready
never
echo
energy
heavy
friend
health
guess
breakfast
fence
stretch
weather
yesterday
desert
sweater
against

Say and Listen

Say each spelling word. Listen for the short *e* sound.

Think and Sort

Look at the letters in each word. Think about how short *e* is spelled. Spell each word aloud.

Short *e* can be shown as /ĕ/. How many spelling patterns for /ĕ/ do you see?

1. Write the nine spelling words that have the *e* pattern.

2. Write the seven spelling words that have the *ea* pattern.

3. Write the two spelling words that have the *ai* pattern.

4. Write the one spelling word that has the *ie* pattern.

5. Write the one spelling word that has the *ue* pattern.

Use the steps on page 4 to study words that are hard for you.

Spelling Patterns

e	ea	ai	ie	ue
fe**n**ce	r**ea**dy	**ai**n	fr**ie**nd	g**ue**ss

www.harcourtschoolsupply.com
14
Lesson 3: Words with Short *e*
Core Skills Spelling 4, SV 9781419034084
© Harcourt Achieve Inc. All rights reserved.

Name: _____   Date: _____

Spelling and Meaning

Antonyms Antonyms are words that have opposite meanings. Write the spelling word that is an antonym of each word.

1. swamp _____
2. sickness _____
3. enemy _____
4. know _____
5. lightweight _____
6. always _____
7. center _____
8. for _____
9. tomorrow _____
10. unprepared _____

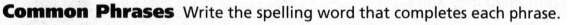

Common Phrases Write the spelling word that completes each phrase.

11. again and _____
12. happily _____ after
13. snowy _____
14. _____ and butter
15. skirt and _____
16. jump over the _____
17. bend and _____
18. the _____ of your voice
19. _____ from the sun

Word Story   Have you ever fasted? To fast is to go a long time without eating. We all fast when we sleep at night. Our first meal of the day breaks, or ends, our fast. Write the spelling word that names this meal.

20. _____

Family Tree: *friend* Think about how the *friend* words are alike in spelling and meaning. Then add another *friend* word to the tree.

friendliness

21. _____

friendlier   unfriendly

friend

Spelling in Context

Use each spelling word once to complete the story.

Seymour Finds a Friend

The autumn _____ was

just right for tennis. Seymour C. Skunk put on

his tennis _____ and shorts.

He ran to the court, feeling full of

_____. He knew that playing

tennis was good for his _____.

Tennis helped him strengthen and

_____ his muscles.

"If only I had someone to play with," Seymour sighed.

"All the other animals always turn up their nose at me. They whisper 'P–U' under their

breath. I would _____ treat someone that way."

Seymour listened to the _____ of his own voice. He felt as though

he were all alone on a _____ island. With a _____ heart,

Seymour gave the ball a smack _____ a wall.

"Great form!" said a young rabbit as she hopped over the _____

around the court.

"How about a game?" Seymour asked.

The rabbit smiled. She followed him to the tennis court. After the game, Seymour

invited the pretty rabbit to have some _____.

"Are you _____ to order?" asked the waiter. He was holding his

nose.

"I will have the forty-carrot muffins," said the rabbit.

"I'll try the spinach surprise. And please bring some French _____,"

said Seymour. He glanced at the rabbit. "What's your name?" he asked.

The rabbit covered her nose with her paws. She gave Seymour quite a start.

"I'm Beatrice Lapin," she answered in a soft voice. "But everyone calls me Bunny."

"You know, Bunny," said Seymour slowly, "_____
15
my life was sad. I didn't think I'd _____ find a
16
_____ like you."
17

Bunny covered her nose _____.
18

Seymour jumped to the _____ of his seat.
19
"There's something I must ask you," he began. "It's a rather 'scent-sitive' subject."

"I know," said Bunny sadly. "You couldn't help but notice that my nose is extremely large."

"Why, Bunny," Seymour said, "I never even noticed your nose. I've been busy thinking my smell was bothering you."

"Why, Seymour, I hadn't even noticed your smell," Bunny smiled and said. "I _____ both of us were busy worrying
20
about ourselves!"

again
edge
bread
ever
ready
never
echo
energy
heavy
friend
health
guess
breakfast
fence
stretch
weather
yesterday
desert
sweater
against

★ Challenge Yourself ★

Challenge Words

kennel	sheriff
cleanse	deafen

Write the Challenge Word for each clue. Check a dictionary to see if you are right. Then use separate paper to write sentences showing that you understand the meaning of each Challenge Word.

21. You should always do this to a cut or scrape before you put on a bandage. _____

22. This person's job is to make sure laws are kept. _____

23. A very loud sound near your ear could do this to you. _____

24. You might say this place has gone to the dogs! _____

Lesson 4

Words with Long *e*

beach

1. *ea* Words

_____
_____
_____
_____
_____
_____
_____
_____
_____
_____
_____

2. *ee* Words

_____
_____
_____
_____
_____
_____
_____
_____
_____

season
knee
queen
scream
reason
between
sweep
sweet
speech
beach
seem
teach
means
speak
freeze
leaf
treat
squeeze
peace
please

Say and Listen

Say each spelling word. Listen for the long e sound.

Think and Sort

Look at the letters in each word. Think about how long e is spelled. Spell each word aloud.

Long e can be shown as /ē/. How many spelling patterns for /ē/ do you see?

1. Write the eleven spelling words that have the *ea* pattern.

2. Write the nine spelling words that have the *ee* pattern.

Use the steps on page 4 to study words that are hard for you.

Spelling Patterns

ea	ee
b**ea**ch	sw**ee**p

© Harcourt Achieve Inc. All rights reserved.
Core Skills Spelling 4, SV 9781419034084

Name: _____ Date: _____

Spelling and Meaning

Classifying Write the spelling word that belongs in each group.

1. dust, vacuum, _____
2. king, princess, _____
3. trunk, branch, _____
4. ankle, thigh, _____
5. shout, yell, _____
6. among, beside, _____
7. sour, salty, _____
8. shows, intends, _____

What's the Answer? Write the spelling word that answers each question.

9. What word do you use to politely ask for something? _____
10. What word names a part of the year? _____
11. What do you give a good dog? _____
12. What word means the same as *talk*? _____
13. What word means "appear to be"? _____
14. What do you call a public talk? _____
15. Where do people go to have fun in the summer sun? _____
16. What do you do to get juice from an orange? _____
17. What tells why something happens? _____
18. If a lake gets cold, what might it do? _____
19. What word means the opposite of *war*? _____

Word **Story** One spelling word was once spelled *taecan*. Later this spelling was changed to *teachen*. The word means "to instruct or to guide in education." Write the spelling we use today.

20. _____

Family Tree: *sweet* Think about how the *sweet* words are alike in spelling and meaning. Then add another *sweet* word to the tree.

sweetly

21. _____

sweetener   sweeter

sweet

Spelling in Context

Use each spelling word once to complete the story.

The Big Race

It was the day of the big race. The track team was having its last meet of the _____. Ella stood with the

1

other runners, waiting for her event. It was the last race of the day.

"I'm scared," she said to her friend Rachel. "Look at me. I'm shaking like a _____."

2

"You're scared?" Rachel squeaked. "I'm so nervous I can hardly _____."

3

"Really? You always _____ so calm," Ella answered.

4

Coach Talbot knelt on one _____ and gave his same old

5

_____ to Ella. "I'll make this short and _____," he said.

6   7

"The one thing I've tried to _____ you is that it's how you play the

8

game that counts. Just because this final race _____ winning the district

9

championship, that's no _____ for you to be scared."

10

Rachel gave Ella's hand a _____, and she whispered, "You can do it!"

11

Ella took her place at the starting line. Suddenly she felt weak. She was afraid that she would _____ up at the starting whistle. She closed her eyes and

12

imagined that she was running along the sandy _____ again. She tried to

13

remember the _____ and quiet of those early mornings.

14

"Starting places, _____," the judge began. "On your mark, get set, . . ."

15

He blew the whistle, and the runners were on their way!

Ella got off to a slow start. As she struggled to speed up, she heard the rest of her team _____, "Go, Ella, Go!" Ella's legs began to move steadily faster.
16

As she rounded the last turn, Ella was ahead of all but three runners. It was time to make her move. With only a few yards left, Ella passed _____ two of the runners in front of her. The crowd began to roar. Ella felt as though she were flying! Soon the front runner began to drop back. She had used up all her energy at the beginning of the race. Ella felt herself _____ past the tired runner and break the tape. Her team had won!
17
18

Coach Talbot jumped for joy and shook Ella's hand. "Fantastic race!" he said to her. Then he looked at the team and said, "Girls, you've earned a _____. I'll take you out for ice cream. You can each have a _____-size cone!"
19
20

"Thanks, coach. You're a sport!" the girls said happily and piled into his car.

season
knee
queen
scream
reason
between
sweep
sweet
speech
beach
seem
teach
means
speak
freeze
leaf
treat
squeeze
peace
please

★ Challenge Yourself ★

Challenge Words

beacon   **conceal**
treason   **meek**

Write the Challenge Word for each clue. Check a dictionary to see if you are right. Then use separate paper to write sentences showing that you understand the meaning of each Challenge Word.

21. When you hide something, you do this to it. _____
22. Someone who is quiet and gentle is this. _____
23. If you help your country's enemies, you are guilty of this crime. _____
24. The light at the top of a lighthouse is this. _____

Lesson 5

Months, Days, and Titles

April

1. Abbreviation
_____

2. One-Syllable Words
_____
_____
_____

3. Two-Syllable Words
_____
_____
_____
_____
_____
_____
_____
_____
_____

4. Three-Syllable Words
_____
_____
_____
_____
_____

5. Four-Syllable Words
_____
_____

October
February
Friday
March
Thursday
December
July
May
Dr.
August
Sunday
June
Monday
September
Tuesday
January
November
Saturday
Wednesday
April

Say and Listen
Say the spelling words. Listen to the sounds in each word.

Think and Sort
Look at the letters in each word. Spell each word aloud.

An **abbreviation** is a shortened form of a word. *Mr.* is an abbreviation for *Mister*.

A **syllable** is a word part with one vowel sound. *Sun* has one syllable. *Sunny* has two syllables.

1. Write the one spelling word that is the abbreviation of *Doctor*.

2. Write the three spelling words that have one syllable.

3. Write the nine spelling words that have two syllables.

4. Write the five spelling words that have three syllables.

5. Write the two spelling words that have four syllables.

Use the steps on page 4 to study words that are hard for you.

Spelling Patterns

One Syllable	Two Syllables
Ma**r**ch	A•pril
Three Syllables	**Four Syllables**
Sep•tem•ber	Jan•u•ar•y

Spelling and Meaning

Clues Write the spelling word for each clue.

1. the month to send valentines _____
2. the first day of the week _____
3. the day after Monday _____
4. the last month of the year _____
5. the first month of autumn _____
6. the first day of the weekend _____
7. the month before December _____
8. the day in the middle of the week _____
9. the month after March _____
10. the first day of the school week _____
11. the month after September _____
12. the day before Friday _____
13. the month between July and September _____
14. a short way to write *Doctor* _____

Rhymes Write the spelling word that completes each sentence and rhymes with the underlined word or words.

15. We can play outside in _____.
16. Will the month of _____ be here soon?
17. Kwan visited the Gateway Arch in _____.
18. I gave Dad a new tie in _____.
19. The new highway will be open on _____.

Word Story Janus was the Roman god of beginnings and endings. He had two faces so that he could see both things. The Romans named the first month after Janus. Write the spelling word that comes from *Janus*.

20. _____

Family Tree: *Sunday* *Sunday* comes from the word *sun*. Think about how the *sun* words are alike in spelling and meaning. Then add another *sun* word to the tree.

sunny

21. _____

Sunday   sunning

sun

Name: _____   Date: _____

The Stories Behind the Names

Have you ever wondered how the days and the months got their names? The first two days of the week were named by people in England hundreds of years ago. They named the first day

_____ to honor the sun.
    1

They called the second day Moon's Day, or

_____, to honor the moon.
    2

The names of the next four days come from ancient Norway. Norwegians named one day Tyr's Day to honor their god, Tyr. Tyr's Day later became known as

_____.
    3

Tyr's father was the god Woden. His day was called Woden's Day, which we now call

_____. Woden had a wife named Frigg. The Norwegians named one day
    4

of the week after her. They called it Frigg's Day, or _____.
                                                              5

The most powerful Norse god was Thor, the god of thunder. We call Thor's Day

_____. The last day of the week, _____, is named for
    6   **7**

Saturn, the ancient Roman god of planting.

The names of our months also come from the ancient Romans, who spoke Latin.

The month of _____ is named for the Roman god Janus. Janus had two
                      8

faces. One face looked into the past. The other looked into the new year. The name of

the second month, _____, comes from the Latin word *februa*, which
                           9

meant "pure." The name of the next month, _____, comes from Mars,
                                                      10

the Roman war god. The Latin word for open was *aprilis*. From *aprilis* comes

_____, the month when flowers open. Maia was the
11

goddess of spring. The month of _____ is named for
12

her. The month of _____ is named for the goddess
13

Juno.

The names of two months come from the names of Roman

emperors. _____ is named for Julius Caesar.
14

_____ is named for Augustus, his nephew.
15

The last four months come from Latin words for the numbers

seven through ten: *septem, octo, novem, decem.* The Roman year started in

March, so the seventh month was _____. The eighth
16

was _____. The ninth was _____, and
17   **18**

the tenth was _____.
19

People have spent years studying words and where they came

from. One of these people is _____ Wilfred Funk. Dr.
20

Funk wrote, "Words truly are little windows through which we can

look into the past." We are grateful to Dr. Funk and people like him

for sharing what they see.

October
February
Friday
March
Thursday
December
July
May
Dr.
August
Sunday
June
Monday
September
Tuesday
January
November
Saturday
Wednesday
April

★ Challenge Yourself ★

Challenge Words

Ms.	Pres.
Gov.	Jr.

Use a dictionary to answer these questions. Then use
separate paper to write sentences showing that you
understand the meaning of each Challenge Word.

21. Is **Ms.** Ana Brown a woman? _____

22. Does the title **Pres.** before a person's name mean that
the person is present? _____

23. What kind of job does **Gov.** Sanchez have? _____

24. Is Jeffrey Smith, **Jr.**, named after his father? _____

Name: _____   Date: _____

Lesson 6

More Words with Long *e*

city

1. *e* Words
_____
_____

2. *y* Words
_____
_____
_____
_____
_____
_____
_____
_____
_____
_____
_____

3. *e*-consonant-*e* Word
_____

4. *eo* Word
_____

5. *i* Words
_____
_____
_____
_____

6. *i*-consonant-*e* Word
_____

people
easy
every
police
radio
zebra
evening
body
family
piano
copy
busy
ski
city
pizza
angry
plenty
hungry
sorry
secret

Say and Listen
Say each spelling word. Listen for the long e sound.

Think and Sort
Look at the letters in each word. Think about how the long e sound is spelled. Spell each word aloud.

Long e can be shown as /ē/. How many spelling patterns for /ē/ do you see?

1. Write the two spelling words that have the e pattern.

2. Write the eleven spelling words that have the y pattern.

3. Write the one spelling word that has the e-consonant-e pattern.

4. Write the one spelling word that has the eo pattern.

5. Write the four spelling words that have the i pattern.

6. Write the one spelling word that has the i-consonant-e pattern.

Use the steps on page 4 to study words that are hard for you.

Spelling Patterns

e z**e**bra	y cit**y**	e-consonant-e **eve**ning
eo p**eo**ple	i sk**i**	i-consonant-e pol**ice**

www.harcourtschoolsupply.com
© Harcourt Achieve Inc. All rights reserved.

Lesson 6: More Words with Long e
Core Skills Spelling 4, SV 9781419034084

Spelling and Meaning

Definitions Write the spelling word for each definition.

1. equipment used to receive sounds sent over airwaves _____
2. something known only to oneself _____
3. government workers who enforce laws _____
4. feeling sadness or pity _____
5. having a lot to do _____
6. to glide across snow or water _____
7. a pie with cheese and tomato sauce _____
8. a striped animal related to the horse _____
9. to make exactly like another _____
10. a center of people and business _____
11. the entire form of a living thing _____

Synonyms Synonyms are words that have the same or almost the same meaning. Write the spelling word that is a synonym for each underlined word.

12. Our homework for tomorrow is simple. _____
13. The teacher gave each student a chore. _____
14. Louis is mad about losing his cap. _____
15. It was a lovely night for a walk. _____
16. Many persons were waiting for the bus. _____
17. We have lots of food for supper. _____
18. Jose's relatives had a reunion last summer. _____
19. I'm starving, so let's eat! _____

Word Story A musical instrument that can be played both softly and loudly was first made in Italy. The instrument became known by the Italian name *pianoforte*, which means "soft and loud." Soon this name was shortened. Write the spelling word that names the instrument.

20. _____

Family Tree: *secret* Think about how the *secret* words are alike in spelling and meaning. Then add another *secret* word to the tree.

secretive

21. _____

secrets

secret

Lesson 6: More Words with Long e
Core Skills Spelling 4, SV 9781419034084

Spelling in Context

Use each spelling word once to complete the selection.

★ ★ Greenville

★ ★ ★ Want Ads ★ ★ ★

Phil Goode Health Club needs teacher for _____ 1 -building class. Help out-of-shape _____ 2 exercise and tone their body. Must be able to do push-ups and jump rope. Must also be able to carry tired customers home. Work hours include four days and one _____ 3 per week. Call I.M. Phitt at 555-5555.

Pop's Parlor needs talented _____ 4 cook who can sing. Must also play the _____ 5 and like preparing mouthwatering food for _____ 6 people. Job requires singing to large crowds. Pop's Parlor is very _____ 7 to reach by bus or train. Call I.E. Talot at 555-4444.

Super Sleuth Seeks Support

Too much work! Helper needed for small but _____ 8 spy business. Must be able to keep a _____ 9 . I offer you _____ 10 of interesting work. Be prepared to work nights and _____ 11 Saturday and Sunday. Office is near center of _____ 12 . Can't tell you where. Send a self-destructing tape to Post Office Box 11 telling why you want the job.

Gazette ★ ★

people
easy
every
police
radio
zebra
evening
body
family
piano
copy
busy
ski
city
pizza
angry
plenty
hungry
sorry
secret

_____ of five with zoo seeks someone
          13
to teach good stable manners to pet _____.
                                                        14
Must really love lizards, bats, elephants, and other unusual pets.
Fax a _____ of a letter from some animal you
              15
have taught to 555-2222. Be sure the letter is signed with a
clear paw print.

★ ★ ★ For Sale ★ ★ ★

Amazing antique AM
_____. Ugly
          16
frame but works perfectly.
Even picks up radio stations
from Antarctica, messages to
_____ cars,
          17
and phone conversations. For
more about this special offer,
call I.M.N. Eavesdropper at
555-6789.

Skiers: Security and Safety on the Slopes

If you've bought cheap poles, don't
get upset or _____ with
                        18
yourself. Buy our no-spills, no-accident
_____ poles. You won't be
          19
_____ you bought them.
          20
Call us before Friday at 555-7890 and get
free book, *Study Guide to Skiing Safety*, and
free pass to any hospital of your choice.

Name: _____ Date: _____

Lesson 7
Words with Short *i*

bridge

1. *a* and *i* Word

_____

2. *a* Word

_____

3. *y* Word

_____

4. *i* Words

_____
_____
_____
_____
_____
_____
_____
_____
_____
_____
_____
_____
_____
_____
_____

5. *ui* Words

_____
_____

quick
deliver
gym
different
picture
middle
interesting
village
written
bridge
guitar
thick
picnic
inch
begin
pitch
itch
chicken
building
package

Say and Listen
Say each spelling word. Listen for the short *i* sound.

Think and Sort
Look at the letters in each word. Think about how short *i* is spelled. Spell each word aloud.

Short *i* can be shown as /ĭ/. How many spelling patterns for /ĭ/ do you see?

1. Write the one spelling word that has the *a* and *i* patterns.

2. Write the one spelling word that has the *a* pattern.

3. Write the one spelling word that has the *y* pattern.

4. Write the fifteen spelling words that have the *i* pattern.

5. Write the two spelling words that have the *ui* pattern.

Use the steps on page 4 to study words that are hard for you.

Spelling Patterns

a	**y**	**i**	**ui**
pack**a**ge	g**y**m	p**i**tch	b**ui**lding

www.harcourtschoolsupply.com
© Harcourt Achieve Inc. All rights reserved.

Lesson 7: Words with Short *i*
Core Skills Spelling 4, SV 9781419034084

Name: _____   Date: _____

Spelling and Meaning

Antonyms Write the spelling word that is an antonym of each underlined word.

1. Michael wants to <u>catch</u> the baseball.   _____
2. Those two pictures are <u>alike</u>.   _____
3. Can we <u>finish</u> reading the story now?   _____
4. Yoshi was <u>slow</u> to finish the job.   _____
5. The gravy was too <u>thin</u>.   _____
6. The movie about whales was
   very <u>boring</u>.   _____
7. I couldn't read the words
   I had <u>erased</u>.   _____
8. The store will <u>receive</u> our
   new furniture.   _____

Classifying Write the spelling word that belongs in each group.

9. duck, goose, _____   10. foot, yard, _____
11. tunnel, arch, _____   12. beginning, end, _____
13. photo, drawing, _____   14. city, town, _____
15. violin, banjo, _____   16. box, carton, _____
17. tickle, scratch, _____   18. making, constructing,
19. cafeteria, classroom,   _____
    _____

Word **Story** The French word *piquenique* once named a gathering of people in which each person brought something to eat. Later the word took on the meaning of "a meal in the open air." Which spelling word names this meal? Write the word.

20. _____

Family Tree: *deliver* Think about how the *deliver* words are alike in spelling and meaning. Then add another *deliver* word to the tree.

undeliverable

21. _____

delivering   delivery

deliver

© Harcourt Achieve Inc. All rights reserved.

Spelling in Context

Use each spelling word once to complete the story.

Scrambled Plans

"Don't forget the eggs!" Mom shouted. Alan and Ling climbed aboard the family spaceship. Ling held her baseball and leaned back in her seat.

"Grocery store," Alan told the spaceship's computer, and the spaceship took off. Then Alan saw a light on the control panel _____ to flash. Alan looked

1
at the computer screen. "Ling, we're not headed for the grocery store. The ship has taken a _____ course!"

2

Two hours later the rocket landed with a bump. Alan and Ling saw that they were in the _____ of some large buildings. Each _____ looked

3   4
like a giant _____ coop. It was a whole _____ of

5   6
chicken coops!

As the children climbed out of the ship, a figure flew toward them as _____ as a flash. Alan and Ling saw that it was a giant chicken. It stood

7
an _____ taller than Alan and had a _____ covering of

8   9
white feathers.

"Welcome, children," he said clearly in English. "We've been EGGS-PECK-ting you! Our great-grandchickens left your planet long ago in search of freedom. Before they left, they made a _____ record of Earth's most

10
_____ sports. One chicken was

11
in charge of boxing and wrapping the record. When our great-grandchickens opened the _____, they found that he had left

12
out the directions for playing the game of baseball!"

"And you want us to teach you?" Ling asked.

32

Name: Date:

"EGGS-actly. Once we learn how to play this great game, we will

_____ 13 you safely back to Earth."

The children agreed, and the chicken flapped his wings with delight. "Follow me," the giant chicken told them. The three crossed

over a _____ 14 and walked until they reached a school

_____ 15 . There Ling and Alan taught the chickens the

lost art of baseball. Ling worked on the _____ 16 , and

Alan worked on the hit.

That evening the chicken planet held its first baseball game.

Everyone brought a _____ 17 supper. Someone played

a _____ 18 throughout the game. Soon the score was

tied 3 to 3. The pitcher was chewing gum and scratching an

_____ 19 on his beak. A high fly over the head of a left-

field chicken ended the game. Alan snapped a _____ 20 of

each team.

"Ling, wake up!" a voice said. It was Alan. "We're at the grocery store. Come on."

"I must have fallen asleep," said Ling. "But I had the most EGG-citing dream!"

quick
deliver
gym
different
picture
middle
interesting
village
written
bridge
guitar
thick
picnic
inch
begin
pitch
itch
chicken
building
package

★ Challenge Yourself ★

Challenge Words
dismal
banish
Gypsy
acknowledge

What do you think each Challenge Word means? Check a dictionary to see if you are right. Then use separate paper to write sentences showing that you understand the meaning of each Challenge Word.

21. We wanted Saturday to be sunny, but the weather was **dismal**.
22. The king decided to **banish** all thieves to an island.
23. Elisa is a **Gypsy**, but her family doesn't travel from place to place.
24. The captain would not **acknowledge** that they were lost.

Lesson 8

Words with Long *i*

lightning

1. *igh* Words
_____
_____
_____
_____
_____
_____
_____
_____
_____
_____
_____
_____
_____

2. *y* Words
_____
_____
_____
_____
_____

3. *ie* Words
_____
_____

night
dry
mighty
tie
fight
flight
right
might
die
spy
midnight
tonight
supply
lightning
reply
highway
high
deny
bright
sight

Say and Listen
Say each spelling word. Listen for the long *i* sound.

Think and Sort
Look at the letters in each word. Think about how long *i* is spelled. Spell each word aloud.

Long *i* can be shown as /ī/. How many spelling patterns for /ī/ do you see?

1. Look at the word *night*. The spelling pattern for this word is *igh*. The *g* and *h* are silent. Write the thirteen spelling words that have the *igh* pattern.

2. Write the five spelling words that have the *y* pattern.

3. Write the two spelling words that have the *ie* pattern.

Use the steps on page 4 to study words that are hard for you.

Spelling Patterns

igh	y	ie
n**igh**t	den**y**	t**ie**

Name: _____ Date: _____

Spelling and Meaning

Analogies Write the spelling word that completes each analogy.

1. *In* is to *out* as *dim* is to _____.
2. *Left* is to_____ as *up* is to *down*.
3. *Weak* is to *helpless* as *strong* is to _____.
4. *Day* is to *light* as _____ is to *dark*.
5. *Rumble* is to *thunder* as *flash* is to _____.
6. *Down* is to *low* as *up* is to _____.
7. *Ear* is to *hearing* as *eye* is to _____.
8. *Gift* is to *present* as *answer* is to _____.
9. *No* is to *yes* as _____ is to *admit*.
10. *Wet* is to _____ as *hot* is to *cold*.

Definitions Write the spelling word for each definition.
Use a dictionary if you need to.

11. the middle of the night   _____
12. to make a bow or knot   _____
13. great strength   _____
14. an airplane trip   _____
15. to struggle   _____
16. to live no more   _____
17. this night   _____
18. the amount available   _____
19. a secret agent   _____

Word Story Long ago England's roads were called ways. Each main road was built higher than the ground around it. What was a main road called? Write the spelling word.

20. _____

Family Tree: *tie* Think about how the *tie* words are alike in spelling and meaning. Then add another *tie* word to the tree.

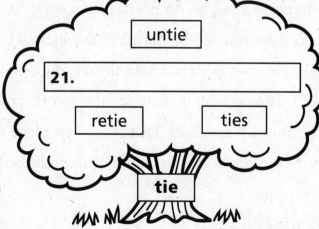

untie

21. _____

retie   ties

tie

© Harcourt Achieve Inc. All rights reserved.
Lesson 8: Words with Long *i*
Core Skills Spelling 4, SV 9781419034084

Spelling in Context

Use each spelling word once to complete the selection.

The Northern Lights

If you ever visit Alaska, you _____ 1 see an amazing

_____ 2. Suppose that the sun has gone down and it is a

dark _____ 3. You are riding in a car down a stretch of

_____ 4. Suddenly there is a flash of light across the sky. It looks

like _____ 5. The flash is so _____ 6 that it lights up

the snow, but the light isn't white. It's green! You wonder if the strange light will

return. It does. Wavy bands of red and purple appear _____ 7 above

the clouds. Long ribbons of light touch the ground. They seem to

_____ 8 the sky to the horizon. You cannot _____ 9

that this is a most unusual sight. What is it? It is the Northern Lights!

Through the ages people have tried to explain the Northern Lights. Long

ago some people believed the Northern Lights were the spirits of animals or birds

in _____ 10. Others said the lights told whether the weather would

be stormy or calm, rainy or _____ 11. Today we know that those

ideas were not _____ 12. They were only interesting stories.

Today people know what the Northern Lights really are. They are caused by

some of the most powerful forces in our solar system. These

_____ 13 forces start on the outside part of the sun. Huge solar flares

shoot up and give off bursts of electricity. This energy shoots toward Earth. The

energy is trapped by Earth's atmosphere. This sudden _____ 14 of

electric energy causes light flashes of green, red, purple, and white.

People who want to see the Northern Lights visit a place that is very far

north, such as Alaska. That is the best place to see them. If a visitor asks an expert

the best way to see the lights, this might be the _____ 15: "First get

away from the lights of the city. Next _____ sleep
₁₆
and try to stay awake. The best lights appear around

_____ . Finally stay until the lights start to
₁₇

_____ out. That is when beautiful clouds of light
₁₈
flash on and off."

Sometimes the Northern Lights stretch down and shine in other

parts of the world. If you look at the sky _____ , you
₁₉

just might _____ a light flash. Who knows? It could
₂₀

be from the Northern Lights!

night
dry
mighty
tie
fight
flight
right
might
die
spy
midnight
tonight
supply
lightning
reply
highway
high
deny
bright
sight

★ Challenge Yourself ★

Challenge Words

eyesight

untimely

dignify

quietness

What do you think each Challenge Word means? Check a
dictionary to see if you are right. Then use the Challenge
Words to write sentences on separate paper.

21. Zack's poor **eyesight** made it difficult for him to
see the board.

23. The **untimely** frost ruined all the fruit on the trees.

24. I won't **dignify** that silly question with a response.

25. The **quietness** of the forest relaxed me.

Name: _____   Date: _____

Lesson 9

More Words with Long *i*

smile

Say and Listen

Say each spelling word. Listen for the long *i* sound.

Think and Sort

Look at the letters in each word. Think about how long *i* is spelled. Spell each word aloud.

Long *i* can be shown as /ī/. How many spelling patterns for /ī/ do you see?

1. Write the twelve spelling words that have the *i*-consonant-*e* pattern.

2. Write the seven spelling words that have the *i* pattern.

3. Write the one spelling word that has the *uy* pattern.

1. *i*-consonant-*e* Words

_____
_____
_____
_____
_____
_____
_____
_____
_____
_____
_____
_____

2. *i* Words

_____
_____
_____
_____
_____
_____
_____

3. *uy* Word

_____

quiet
buy
life
knife
giant
climb
awhile
sunshine
smile
blind
slide
beside
twice
write
surprise
behind
child
size
wise
iron

Use the steps on page 4 to study words that are hard for you.

Spelling Patterns

i-consonant-e	i	uy
life	child	buy

© Harcourt Achieve Inc. All rights reserved.

Name: _____   Date: _____

Spelling and Meaning

Definitions Write the spelling word for each definition.

1. something that happens without warning _____
2. of great size _____
3. the light of the sun _____
4. in back of _____
5. with little or no noise _____
6. next to _____
7. a metal tool used to press wrinkled fabric _____
8. for a brief time _____
9. an instrument used for cutting _____

Rhymes Write the spelling word that completes each sentence and rhymes with the underlined word.

10. It's hard to _____ for a long <u>while</u>.
11. What _____ are the <u>pies</u> you baked?
12. She was so <u>nice</u> to call me _____.
13. He had a <u>wife</u> for forty years of his _____.
14. Let's _____ Dad the yellow <u>tie</u>.
15. The _____ had a <u>mild</u> cold.
16. Mike and Ike <u>tried</u> to _____ down the hill.
17. It will take a long <u>time</u> to _____ that mountain.
18. It is _____ not to tell <u>lies</u>.
19. The children were <u>kind</u> to the _____ bird.

Word Story   The Old English word *writan* meant "to outline or draw a figure of." Later the word meant "to set down in writing." Write the spelling word that comes from *writan*.

20. _____

Family Tree: *quiet* Think about how the *quiet* words are alike in spelling and meaning. Then add another *quiet* word to the tree.

quieted

21. _____

quietness   quieter

quiet

www.harcourtschoolsupply.com
© Harcourt Achieve Inc. All rights reserved.

Lesson 9: More Words with Long *i*
Core Skills Spelling 4, SV 9781419034084

Spelling in Context

Use each spelling word once to complete the selection.

Born to Dig!

Moles are fat little mammals that live underground. People hardly ever see them. These busy animals spend their whole _____ underground.
                                                 1

A mole is made for digging. It has a pointed nose and a V-shaped head. Its ears do not stick out, so it can _____ easily through the
                                    2
soil. The mole's fur flattens in either direction to allow the mole to go forward or backward in its tunnel.

The mole's best digging tools are its huge front paws. They are as strong as _____! The paws have sharp claws that cut through the soil. Then the
                              3
mole uses the flat part of its paws to sweep the soil _____ it. As the mole
                                                                        4
digs, its paws move back and forth so quickly that the mole looks like a young _____ splashing in water. Moles live where there is no
                          5
_____. Sight, however, is not important to moles. Moles have very tiny
              6
eyes and are almost _____.
                                        7

A mole's pink mouth may have a curve that looks like a perky little _____, but this animal is not friendly at all. In fact, it likes to be alone. It
              8
is a fierce fighter, too. A small animal that falls into its tunnel is sure to get an unhappy _____. The mole senses its movement and rushes to attack. The mole
              9
grabs the prey with its two extra-long teeth. Each curved tooth is as sharp as a _____.
              10

Most moles are between five and eight inches long. Russian moles, however, are nearly _____ that _____! These _____
              11   **12**   **13**

moles are very good swimmers. They like to build their tunnels
_____ a pond or river.
14

If you want to see a mole, look for a meadow that has cone-
shaped molehills. Find or _____ some earthworms to
15
drop into the mole's tunnel. Then be very still and
_____. Sit there _____. If you are
16 **17**
lucky, a mole will _____ up to the tunnel entrance.
18
Just remember that it is not _____ to touch a mole. Its
19
teeth and claws can hurt you!

Would you like to learn more about moles? All you need to do is
visit a library or _____ to a government wildlife
20
agency for information.

Word box (spiral notepad):
quiet
buy
life
knife
giant
climb
awhile
sunshine
smile
blind
slide
beside
twice
write
surprise
behind
child
size
wise
iron

★ Challenge Yourself ★

Challenge Words

acquire	**collide**
defiant	**revive**

What do you think each Challenge Word means? Check a
dictionary to see if you are right. Then use separate paper
to write sentences showing that you understand
the meaning of each Challenge Word.

21. Andy needs to earn money in order to **acquire** a new bicycle.
22. The hall is so crowded that students sometimes **collide**.
23. Rita thought her dog was **defiant** because he did not follow her commands.
24. The droopy flowers began to **revive** after the rain.

Lesson 10

Plural Words

foxes

1. *-s* Plurals

_____
_____
_____
_____
_____
_____

2. *-es* Plurals

_____
_____
_____
_____
_____
_____
_____
_____
_____

3. *-ies* Plurals

_____
_____
_____
_____
_____

brothers
families
dishes
trees
pennies
classes
pockets
cities
buses
brushes
rocks
babies
inches
branches
hikes
peaches
stories
foxes
boxes
gloves

Say and Listen

Say the spelling words. Listen to the sounds at the end of each word.

Think and Sort

All of the spelling words are plurals. **Plurals** are words that name more than one thing. Look at the spelling words. Think about how each plural was formed. Spell each word aloud.

1. Most plurals are formed by adding *-s* to the base word. Write the six spelling words that are formed by adding *-s.*

2. Some plurals are formed by adding *-es* to the base word. Write the nine spelling words that are formed by adding *-es.*

3. If a word ends in a consonant and *y*, the *y* is changed to *i* before *-es* is added. Write the five spelling words that are formed by dropping *y* and adding *-ies.*

Use the steps on page 4 to study words that are hard for you.

Spelling Patterns

-s	-es	-ies
tree**s**	inch**es**	cit**ies**
rock**s**	class**es**	stor**ies**

Name: _____ Date: _____

Spelling and Meaning

Classifying Write the spelling word that belongs in each group.

1. planes, trains, _____
2. villages, towns, _____
3. pebbles, stones, _____
4. fathers, uncles, _____
5. dimes, nickels, _____

6. jars, cans, _____
7. yards, feet, _____
8. dogs, wolves, _____

9. leaves, twigs, _____
10. adults, children, _____
11. tales, legends, _____

What's the Answer? Write the spelling word that answers each question.

12. What do mothers, fathers, and children belong to? _____
13. On what do apples and oranges grow? _____
14. What holds coins, wallets, and other things? _____
15. What are long walks on foot? _____
16. If it's cold, what do you wear on your hands? _____
17. On what do people serve food? _____
18. What do teachers call groups of students? _____
19. What do you use on your hair and your teeth? _____

Word Story One of the spelling words is the name of a fruit. The Romans called this fruit a Persian apple, or *persicum malum*. The French changed the word to *pesche*. It is from *pesche* that the word came into English. Write the spelling word.

20. _____

Family Tree: classes *Classes* is a form of *class*. Think about how the *class* words are alike in spelling and meaning. Then add another *class* word to the tree.

classes

21. _____

classify   classic

class

Spelling in Context

Use each spelling word once to complete the story.

A Dream Come True

I'd always wanted to climb Harris Mountain. I'd

taken _____ in mountain climbing
                1

and had gone up small peaks with Jason and

Michael. They were like _____ to
                                 2

me. Now we were finally going to climb the tallest

mountain around these parts.

Jason, Michael, and I left early, driving through

several neighboring _____ and
                            3

towns. Along the way I could hear the hum of the

motors in cars and _____. Finally
                            4

we arrived.

Michael said, "Come on, Small Fry."

I went, but I wanted to tell him I was tired of

being called Small Fry. We strapped ourselves together and put on our

_____. I was between Michael and Jason because I cannot see.
        5

The climb began well. The base of the mountain had lots of pines. Their

_____ felt like the bristles of _____ against my face.
        6   7

Michael described the animals he saw as we climbed—some _____
                                                                          8

and two rabbit _____! I heard screeching sounds, which Jason said
                        9

came from a red-tailed hawk. We figured that her _____ were in a
                                                              10

nest nearby. We rested on a ledge and told _____ about exciting
                                                      11

_____ we'd taken. We opened our _____ of raisins
        12   13

and nuts. Michael took out the three _____ he'd packed, and we
                                              14

began eating.

44

"One good thing about this lunch is that there are no

_____ to wash," I joked.
        15

Soon we began to climb again. Now there were no more pine

_____, just hard _____. Suddenly I felt
        16   17

the rocks crumble beneath me and I fell. I lost all sense of where I was

and thrashed my arms and legs wildly, trying to grab onto something.

Then I remembered to stay calm.

"Are you OK?" Jason asked, holding the rope.

"Just a few more _____ up with your right foot!"
                            18

Michael shouted.

At last I got my footing.

"Some rock slide!" yelled Michael. "Nice work, Nick!"

The rest of the way up the mountain was easier. At the top I

searched my _____ until I found the three lucky
                    19

_____ that Jason had given me, knowing that it was
        20

more than luck that got us to the top. I placed the coins on the ground

as proof that we were there.

Somehow I knew, too, that they would never call me Small Fry

again.

Word list:
brothers
families
dishes
trees
pennies
classes
pockets
cities
buses
brushes
rocks
babies
inches
branches
hikes
peaches
stories
foxes
boxes
gloves

★ Challenge Yourself ★

Challenge Words
utensils
draperies
skiers
festivities

What do you think each Challenge Word means? Check a dictionary to see if you are right. Then use separate paper to write sentences showing that you understand the meaning of each Challenge Word.

21. Fog hid the mountain like **draperies** covering a window.

22. Many **skiers** race down the mountain slopes after it snows.

23. Our only cooking **utensils** were a pan and a spoon.

24. The party's **festivities** included singing and special foods.

Lesson 11 | Words with Short *o*

doctor

1. *o* Words

_____
_____
_____
_____
_____
_____
_____
_____
_____
_____
_____
_____
_____
_____
_____
_____

2. *a* Words

_____
_____
_____
_____

hobby
wash
model
forgot
doctor
contest
object
o'clock
wallet
cotton
dollar
solve
watch
knock
problem
bottom
swallow
beyond
knot
hospital

Say and Listen

Say each spelling word. Listen for the short *o* sound.

Think and Sort

Look at the letters in each word. Think about how short *o* is spelled. Spell each word aloud.

Short *o* can be shown as /ŏ/. How many spelling patterns for /ŏ/ do you see?

1. Write the sixteen spelling words that have the *o* pattern.

2. Write the four spelling words that have the *a* pattern.

Use the steps on page 4 to study words that are hard for you.

Spelling Patterns

o	**a**
s**o**lve	w**a**sh

Spelling and Meaning

Classifying Write the spelling word that belongs in each group.

1. sparrow, wren, _____
2. tap, _____, bang
3. clean, scrub, _____
4. see, _____, observe
5. dime, quarter, _____
6. unscramble, answer, _____
7. _____, silk, wool
8. race, game, _____
9. goal, _____, purpose
10. billfold, _____, purse
11. example, _____, copy
12. past, over, _____

What's the Answer? Write the spelling word that answers each question.

13. Whom do people call when they are sick? _____
14. What is the opposite of *remembered*? _____
15. What word means "of the clock"? _____
16. What can be tied in a rope or cord? _____
17. What is the opposite of *top*? _____
18. Stamp collecting is an example of what? _____
19. What comes before a solution? _____

Word Story   *Hospitale* was a Latin word that meant "guesthouse." Write the spelling word that comes from *hospitale* and now means "a place where sick people go to get well."

20. _____

Family Tree: *wash* Think about how the *wash* words are alike in spelling and meaning. Then add another *wash* word to the tree.

washer

21. _____

rewash   washable

wash

Name: _____ Date: _____

Spelling in Context

Use each spelling word once to complete the story.

A Hobby for Angela

My sister just built a _____ of a ship. Building models is her

_____. My brother likes to work with leather. He made a beautiful

_____ last week. Dad gave him a _____ to put in it.

Dad was happy because he finally won a _____. He's always entering

them. I thought the contest he won was silly. Dad wrote 25 words about why he likes

to do the _____ with new blue Cleano. And Mom? She likes to

_____ birds. She was very excited Monday when she saw a

_____.

I'm the only one in my family who doesn't have a hobby. Everyone else has one

thing that he or she loves to do. My _____ is that I like everything. It

seems a shame to spend all my time on one activity. There are so many interesting

things to do. Yesterday I even got into a "scrape" trying to _____ my

hobby problem.

It all started when I thought skating

might be my hobby. I was rolling down

Holly Hill and had just picked up speed.

The wind felt wonderful against my face.

Then I saw someone flying a kite at the

park. The kite was made of bright blue

_____ fabric. Red tails were

waving below it. Each tail had a bow-tie

_____ tied at the end of it.

I _____ all about skating. I

thought about how much fun flying kites

would be as a hobby. Before I knew it, I was at the

_____ of the hill. Just _____ the
                  14   15

bottom is a sharp turn. Well, the road turned, but I didn't. CRASH!

My right knee got quite a _____, and I got a scrape
                                        16

on my chin.

    Mom wasn't too happy when the police officer called her at

two _____. She left her office and met us at the
           17

_____. At first she was angry with me. Then she
        18

told me she was only angry because she was frightened. The

_____ cleaned my scrape and bandaged my knee.
        19

She told me to wash my chin with special medicine. I didn't

_____. My chin hurt, and I wanted to get better.
        20

    It was an exciting day, though. I got to see lots of doctors and

nurses. The inside of a hospital is really interesting. I told the doctor

how much I liked visiting the hospital. Mom couldn't stop laughing

when the doctor said, "Just don't make it a hobby!"

hobby
wash
model
forgot
doctor
contest
object
o'clock
wallet
cotton
dollar
solve
watch
knock
problem
bottom
swallow
beyond
knot
hospital

★ Challenge Yourself ★

Challenge Words

squad	exotic
apricot	volcanic

Use a dictionary to answer the questions. Then use separate paper to write sentences showing that you understand the meaning of each Challenge Word.

21. Would you expect to find a **squad** of players on a field during a football game? _____

22. Would you expect to see **exotic** birds and animals from around the world at a famous zoo? _____

23. Does an **apricot** look like a banana? _____

24. After the fire goes out, would you expect to find **volcanic** ashes in your fireplace? _____

Lesson 12
Words with Long *o*

pony

1. *o* Words
_____
_____
_____
_____
_____
_____
_____
_____
_____
_____
_____
_____
_____

2. *oa* Words
_____
_____
_____
_____
_____

3. *oe* Words
_____
_____

clothes
total
oak
ocean
obey
throat
pony
poem
coach
coast
goes
almost
only
comb
motor
hotel
soap
zero
toe
program

Say and Listen
Say each spelling word. Listen for the long *o* sound.

Think and Sort
Look at the letters in each word. Think about how long *o* is spelled. Spell each word aloud.

Long *o* can be shown as /ō/. How many spelling patterns for /ō/ do you see?

1. Write the thirteen spelling words that have the *o* pattern.

2. Write the five spelling words that have the *oa* pattern.

3. Write the two spelling words that have the *oe* pattern.

Use the steps on page 4 to study words that are hard for you.

Spelling Patterns

o	**oa**	**oe**
zer**o**	s**oa**p	g**oe**s

Spelling and Meaning

Synonyms Write the spelling word that is a synonym
for each underlined word.

1. This <u>shoreline</u> is rocky and steep.   _____
2. Wally <u>nearly</u> lost the race.   _____
3. You must <u>follow</u> the rules to play.   _____
4. The <u>sum</u> was more than fifty dollars.   _____
5. Collin <u>travels</u> everywhere by bus.   _____
6. The <u>sea</u> here is very blue.   _____
7. Ramon had <u>just</u> five dollars left.   _____
8. What is your favorite TV <u>show</u>?   _____

Clues Write the spelling word for each clue.

9. People wash with this.   _____
10. Ten minus ten equals this.   _____
11. This is a place for travelers to stay.   _____
12. This is a small horse.   _____
13. You can use this to make your hair neat.   _____
14. This can get sore when you get a cold.   _____
15. This can rhyme.   _____
16. This is found on your foot.   _____
17. This is a kind of tree.   _____
18. This person trains athletes.   _____
19. People wear these.   _____

Word Story   Many English
words come from Latin. One of the
spelling words and the word *move*
come from the same Latin word,
movere. The spelling word names a
machine that causes things to move.
Write the word.

20. _____

Family Tree: *comb* Think about how
the *comb* words are alike in spelling and
meaning. Then add another *comb* word to
the tree.

uncombed

21. _____

combed   combs

comb

Name: _____   Date: _____

Spelling in Context

Use each spelling word once to complete the selection.

Vacation Mail

Dear Grandma,

We've been on vacation in Grand Cayman for _____ 1 a week now.

Our _____ 2 is nice. They give you little bars of face

_____ 3 and little bottles of shampoo.

The most fun I've had so far is snorkeling in the _____ 4. Dad

decided to take me with him after we'd been here for _____ 5 one day.

I had to promise to _____ 6 the safety rules at all times! Dad taught me

how to move the funny rubber feet. Then I learned to breathe through a snorkel.

Later that afternoon, we went along the _____ 7 by boat to a

coral reef. When we turned the _____ 8 off and stopped the boat, Dad

and another diver jumped over the side. Then I went in, yelling, "Here

_____ 9 nothing!"

I swam near the surface. A beautiful angelfish swam right in front of my face. A

canary fish brushed my side. My feeling was one of _____ 10 wonder. I

am going to write a _____ 11 about swimming with the fish.

Dad had to drag me out of the water. Then

we changed out of our swimsuits and into our

_____ 12 and got the other diver

to take a picture of us. Can you tell that we

forgot to _____ 13 our hair? I

got a sore _____ 14, but it was

worth it!

Love,

Tracy

Name: Date:

Dear Tracy,

How lucky you are to be on Grand Cayman! This morning
the temperature here fell to _____, and my old
                                    15
_____ tree is totally covered with snow.
      16
Outside, Mr. Johnson's _____ is puffing his
                              17
white breath into the air. I am stuck indoors for a while—I
tripped and broke my _____ yesterday.
                            18
I loved your letter. The picture of you and your dad is very
funny! I'll bet snorkeling is really fun. I've never been, but I
watched a _____ about it on television last
                  19
month.

Well, hurry home! I found out I will be the
_____ of the Hillsboro soccer team. We start
      20
practice next week. By then I will be able to walk. Why not come
with me to practice?

Love you,
Grandma

| clothes |
| total |
| oak |
| ocean |
| obey |
| throat |
| pony |
| poem |
| coach |
| coast |
| goes |
| almost |
| only |
| comb |
| motor |
| hotel |
| soap |
| zero |
| toe |
| program |

★ Challenge Yourself ★

Challenge Words

| appropriate | host |
| enclosure | foe |

Write the correct Challenge Word for each clue. Check a
dictionary to see if you are right. Then use separate paper
to write sentences showing that you understand the
meaning of each Challenge Word.

21. You can use this to keep a pet from running away. _____
22. This word rhymes with *ghost* and means "a person who
entertains guests." _____
23. An enemy is this. _____
24. If you dress warmly on a very cold day, then your clothing
is this. _____

Lesson 13
More Words with Long *o*

window

Say and Listen

Say each spelling word. Listen for the long *o* sound.

Think and Sort

Look at the letters in each word. Think about how long *o* is spelled. Spell each word aloud.

Long *o* can be shown as /ō/. How many spelling patterns for /ō/ do you see?

1. Write the nine spelling words that have the *o*-consonant-*e* pattern.

2. Write the ten spelling words that have the *ow* pattern.

3. In the *ough* spelling pattern, the *g* and the *h* are silent. Write the one spelling word that has the *ough* pattern.

Use the steps on page 4 to study words that are hard for you.

1. *o-consonant-e* Words
_____
_____
_____
_____
_____
_____
_____
_____
_____

2. *ow* Words
_____
_____
_____
_____
_____
_____
_____
_____
_____
_____

3. *ough* Word
_____

below
elbow
froze
alone
broke
though
knows
pillow
own
explode
hollow
chose
shadow
close
nose
those
slowly
tomorrow
stole
window

Spelling Patterns

o-consonant-**e**	**ow**	**ough**
br**oke**	**ow**n	th**ough**

Name: _____   Date: _____

Spelling and Meaning

Antonyms   Write the spelling word that is an antonym of each underlined word.

1. The trunk of the oak tree was <u>solid</u>.   _____
2. Dad <u>fixed</u> the new window.   _____
3. Will you please <u>open</u> the door?   _____
4. The car drove <u>quickly</u> past the house.   _____
5. Aunt Cleo <u>thawed</u> the turkey.   _____
6. Todd's apartment is <u>above</u> Yuri's.   _____
7. Let's do the assignment <u>together</u>.   _____

Analogies   Write the spelling word that completes each analogy.

8. *Eat* is to *ate* as *steal* is to _____.
9. *Board* is to *hard* as _____ is to *soft*.
10. *Leg* is to *knee* as *arm* is to _____.
11. *Sing* is to *sang* as *choose* is to _____.
12. *Yesterday* is to *past* as _____ is to *future*.
13. *Taste* is to *mouth* as *smell* is to _____.
14. *Says* is to *speaks* as _____ is to *understands*.
15. *Match* is to *burn* as *firecracker* is to _____.
16. *Dark* is to _____ as *smooth* is to *silk*.
17. *Hard* is to *difficult* as *have* is to _____.
18. *This* is to *that* as *these* is to _____.
19. *Also* is to *too* as _____ is to *however*.

Word Story   One of the spelling words comes from the old Viking word *vindauga*. *Vindauga* meant "wind-eye." A *vindauga* was an opening, through which the wind might enter a house. Today this opening is often covered with glass. Write the word.

20. _____

Family Tree: *own*   Think about how the *own* words are alike in spelling and meaning. Then add another *own* word to the tree.

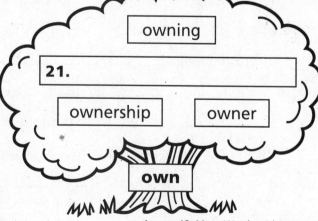

owning

21. _____

ownership   owner

own

© Harcourt Achieve Inc. All rights reserved.
Lesson 13: More Words with Long *o*
Core Skills Spelling 4, SV 9781419034084

Name: _____   Date: _____

Spelling in Context

Use each spelling word once to complete the story.

Pop's Old Barn

The old barn on the Wilson farm stood on

the hilltop and cast a long black

_____. Moonlight streaming
                1

through each _____ made it
                    2

look like a _____ head. People
                  3

said that the barn was haunted. Young John

Wilson agreed. "Count me out if you're going

to Pop's old barn," he told his friends.

"I don't think that place is scary," B.J. said. "Do you, Sarah?"

"No, I don't," Sarah answered firmly.

"I want to explore the barn _____ night. Who's going with me?"
                                          4

asked B.J.

Sarah thought for a minute, and then _____ to join B.J. "I will!"
                                                      5

she replied.

But John said, "I wish my pop would tear it down. Count me out."

Late the next evening, B.J. and Sarah quietly _____ through the
                                                              6

Wilson land to the barn. _____ they removed a wooden bolt from the
                                    7

door. The squeaking noise made their skin crawl. Standing very _____
                                                                               8

together, they tiptoed through the pitch-black room. Rustling noises came from in

front of them.

"I wonder what _____ noises are," B.J. said. Then he felt something
                        9

brush his shoe. He _____ in his tracks. His hands felt as
                            10

_____ they were made of ice. "Something just hit my foot," he whispered.
        11

"It was probably just a mouse," Sarah said shakily. Then she looked around. "Maybe we

should go home," she told B.J. "Who _____ what's inside this place?"
                                                12

www.harcourtschoolsupply.com
© Harcourt Achieve Inc. All rights reserved.

56

Lesson 13: More Words with Long o
Core Skills Spelling 4, SV 9781419034084

"No, let's go on," B.J. said. "I want to find out if this place is really haunted." He took Sarah by an _____ and led her to a ladder just _____ the loft.
    13
                          14

As they began to climb, they heard a crack. A rung of the ladder _____ beneath B.J.'s foot, sending him falling to the
    15
ground. He dusted himself off and got up. "Look!" he cried.

A strange purple light was circling the room. B.J. and Sarah stared at a pale white face as a wild laugh filled the barn.

"Help!" Sarah screamed. Then she ran like a scared rabbit.

B.J. answered with a scream of his _____. "Sarah,
                                  16
don't leave me here _____!" His voice seemed to
                   17
_____ from inside him. He shot toward the door.
    18
Suddenly the white face was right in front of him!

"Hey, guys, it's me!" said John. He tossed off a white case from a _____. In it he had cut holes for his eyes and
    19
_____. He circled his flashlight once more around
    20
the room.

"Was I pretty scary?" he asked with a laugh.

B.J. and Sarah looked at each other and giggled. "Yes!" they said together. "Too scary!"

below
elbow
froze
alone
broke
though
knows
pillow
own
explode
hollow
chose
shadow
close
nose
those
slowly
tomorrow
stole
window

★ Challenge Yourself ★

Challenge Words

bouquet	dispose
stow	sow

What do you think each Challenge Word means? Check a dictionary to see if you are right. Then use separate paper to write sentences showing that you understand the meaning of each Challenge Word.

21. The flowers were made into a beautiful **bouquet**.

22. Please use the garbage can to **dispose** of your trash.

23. Passengers must **stow** their suitcases under their seats or in a closet.

24. In spring we **sow** grass seed on our front lawn.

Name: _____   Date: _____

Lesson 14

Words with Short *u*

jungle

1. *u* Words

_____
_____
_____
_____
_____
_____
_____
_____
_____
_____
_____

2. *ou* Words

_____
_____
_____
_____
_____
_____
_____
_____

3. *oe* Word

_____

suddenly
rough
knuckle
trouble
touch
brush
couple
button
does
fudge
hunt
enough
tough
country
until
double
subject
under
jungle
hundred

Say and Listen

Say each spelling word. Listen for the short *u* sound.

Think and Sort

Look at the letters in each word. Think about how short *u* is spelled. Spell each word aloud.

Short *u* can be shown as /ŭ/. How many spelling patterns for /ŭ/ do you see?

1. Write the eleven spelling words that have the *u* pattern.

2. Write the eight spelling words that have the *ou* pattern.

3. Write the one spelling word that has the *oe* pattern.

Use the steps on page 4 to study words that are hard for you.

Spelling Patterns

u	ou	oe
h**u**nt	t**ou**ch	d**oe**s

Spelling and Meaning

Hink Pinks Hink pinks are pairs of rhyming words that have a funny meaning. Read each meaning. Write the spelling word that completes each hink pink.

1. grooming the hair in a hurry _____ rush
2. things made out of sandpaper _____ stuff
3. looking for a daring trick to do   stunt _____
4. person choosing the best candy _____ judge
5. something that fastens fingers together _____ buckle
6. twins who always cause problems _____ trouble
7. a piece of meat that is hard to chew _____ stuff

What's the Answer? Write the spelling word that answers each question.

8. What is the opposite of *over*? _____
9. Which word is a form of *do*? _____
10. What is science or math an example of? _____
11. Which word means "up to the time of"? _____
12. What is Canada? _____
13. How many pennies are in a dollar? _____
14. What can you call two things? _____
15. What is another word for *difficulty*? _____
16. To which sense do fingers belong? _____
17. Which word means "to happen without warning"? _____
18. What do you have when you have all you need? _____
19. What place is hot and wet? _____

Word Story   The French word for a flower bud is *bouton*. One spelling word comes from *bouton*. It names a knob that pushes through a buttonhole like a flower bud pushes through leaves. Write the spelling word.

20. _____

Family Tree: *rough* Think about how the *rough* words are alike in spelling and meaning. Then add another *rough* word to the tree.

rougher

21.

roughened   roughen

rough

Lesson 14: Words with Short *u*
Core Skills Spelling 4, SV 9781419034084

Spelling in Context

Use each spelling word once to complete the story.

The Oral Report

Jenna was scared. She stared at the clock in Mr. Olivero's room. Only twenty more

minutes _____ lunch! By then all this would be over.
      1

"Maybe he'll forget about it," Jenna wished. "I'll bet there isn't _____
                                                                              2

time to hear everyone today, anyway."

Jenna started to _____ through her desk for her notes. Mr. Olivero
                        3

began, "The _____ of this week's geography lesson is South America.
                  4

We are going to hear some reports from our Brazil team. _____ the team
                                                                  5

have everything in order?"

"Yes, Mr. Olivero," said Patrick Johnson.

Jenna stared down at her notes. It was almost her turn. One of her fingernails felt

_____. She chewed it nervously.
      6

Jenna felt Patrick _____ past her as he stepped to the front of the
                          7

room. She was surprised to see Patrick's hands shaking. Poor Patrick was holding his notes

so tightly that each _____ on his hands was white!
                            8

"Brazil," he began. "Brazil is the largest _____ in South America.
                                                    9

Its population is more than _____ that of other South American
                                  10

countries. . . ."

Jenna barely heard Patrick's speech as she nervously played with a loose

_____ on her dress. She thought about the big piece of
      11

_____ cake that she would eat at lunch. Jenna looked at the clock again.
      12

In a _____ of minutes, the bell would ring.
            13

"Very nice, Patrick. And now, we will hear from Jenna about the Amazon River."

Jenna's heart pounded. Her wet, shaking hands reached _____ her
                                                                    14

desk for the map she had made for the report.

"Oh, no. Where's my map?" she wondered. "I guess I'm really in

_____ now!" _____ she felt her
         15   **16**

fingers _____ the map. Jenna stepped to the front of
              17

the room.

"The Amazon River begins

in the Andes Mountains and flows

eastward through Brazil," she said

loudly. "More than two

_____ small rivers
         18

flow into the Amazon. Much of

the land along the river is

_____ . . . ."
         19

Before she knew it, the report

was done and the bell rang. Patrick ran up to Jenna. "That wasn't as

_____ as we thought it would be!" he told her.
         20

Then Anna Ramos joined them. "Hey, guys. You were great! Were

you scared?"

"Are you kidding?" laughed Jenna. "It was nothing!"

suddenly
rough
knuckle
trouble
touch
brush
couple
button
does
fudge
hunt
enough
tough
country
until
double
subject
under
jungle
hundred

★ Challenge Yourself ★

Challenge Words

customary
countryside
erupt
construct

Use a dictionary to answer the questions. Then use separate paper to write sentences showing that you understand the meaning of each Challenge Word.

21. Is it **customary** for students to study for tests at a
     party? _____

22. Would a book about volcanoes probably tell why
     they **erupt**? _____

23. Would it be wise to **construct** a boat out of paper? _____

24. Would the **countryside** be a good place to find insects and wildflowers?

_____

Lesson 15 Contractions

couldn't

1. Contractions with *not*

_____
_____
_____
_____
_____
_____
_____
_____
_____
_____
_____
_____

2. Other Contractions

a. _____
b. _____
c. _____
d. _____
e. _____
f. _____
g. _____
h. _____

that's
she'd
they've
weren't
doesn't
isn't
wouldn't
wasn't
aren't
we're
you'd
don't
I'm
hadn't
haven't
didn't
shouldn't
let's
couldn't
they'll

Say and Listen

Say the spelling words. Listen to the ending sounds.

Think and Sort

All of the spelling words are contractions. A **contraction** is a short way to write two or more words. The words are joined, but one or more letters are left out. An apostrophe (') is used in place of the missing letters. Look at each spelling word. Think about what the second word in the contraction is. Spell each word aloud.

1. Write the twelve spelling words that are contractions formed with *not*.

2. Solve these contraction puzzles to write eight spelling words.

   a. I + am =   **b.** that + is =

   c. we + are =   **d.** let + us =

   e. they + have =   **f.** you + would =

   g. she + had =   **h.** they + will =

Use the steps on page 4 to study words that are hard for you.

Spelling Patterns

| do + n**ot** = don't | they + **ha**ve = they've | you + **ha**d = you'd
you + **woul**d = you'd |

Spelling and Meaning

Rhymes Write the spelling word that completes each sentence and rhymes with the underlined word.

1. When the bells <u>chime</u>, _____ going home.
2. The team made a <u>save</u>, and now _____ won!
3. She said that _____ <u>need</u> your help.
4. Soon _____ going to move <u>near</u> you.
5. Maybe _____ like to eat Chinese <u>food</u>.
6. After the sun <u>sets</u>, _____ take a walk.
7. Tomorrow _____ pick up the <u>mail</u>.
8. I guess _____ the last of the <u>hats</u>.
9. They _____ going to eat <u>burnt</u> toast.

have + not =

would + not =

I + am =

Trading Places Write the spelling word that can take the place of the underlined words in each sentence.

10. Wanda <u>did not</u> plan a fancy party.   _____
11. We <u>do not</u> want to argue.   _____
12. This pen <u>does not</u> leak.   _____
13. The bus <u>was not</u> on time today.   _____
14. The students <u>have not</u> eaten lunch yet.   _____
15. I <u>would not</u> try to trick you.   _____
16. You <u>should not</u> forget to brush your teeth. _____
17. Broccoli <u>is not</u> my favorite vegetable.   _____
18. My parents <u>are not</u> able to go to the meeting. _____
19. We <u>had not</u> seen the new baby before today.   _____

Word Story
Verbs have different forms for present, past, and future actions. A form of the verb *can* used to be spelled *colde*. Guess how we spell *colde* today. Then add *not* and write the contraction.

20. _____

Family Tree: *would*
Think about how the *would* contractions are alike in spelling and meaning. Then add another *would* contraction to the tree.

I'd   we'd

21. _____

they'd   she'd

would

Spelling in Context

Use each spelling word once to complete the story.

Pecos Bill

It _____ every day that a boy grows up with coyotes. But then,
1

Pecos Bill _____ an everyday fellow. When he just was a baby, Bill
2

drank mountain lion's milk. _____ think that this would be hard to
3

get! But for Bill's mother, it was a snap. Why, _____ fight off an army
4

single-handed!

Pecos Bill's father was one of the first to settle Texas, back when there

_____ many people around. But when people started settling just fifty
5

miles away, he knew it was time to go! "It's too crowded around here," he said.

"_____ pack up our things. _____ going west."
6   7

The family piled into a wagon, with baby Bill in the back. As they crossed the

Pecos River, a large bump sent Bill flying out of the wagon! He _____
8

call out for help. Bill's family _____ notice he was gone until four
9

weeks later. By that time it was winter, and his family couldn't go back to look for him.

"Surely some people found him," his father said. "_____ take good care
10

of him."

Bill was taken in by a pack of coyotes.
For ten happy years, he lived among them.
Because he _____ seen any
11

people, Bill was sure that he was one of

the coyotes.

One day a cowboy came riding along

and spotted Bill and his pet mountain lion

fighting a bear. The cowboy talked to Bill.

He promised that he _____
12

hurt Bill, but Bill couldn't understand him. The cowboy taught Bill

to speak. "You _____ a coyote," he told Bill one day.
        13
"You're a boy."

        "No, _____ a coyote!" Bill said. "Listen. I can
                14
howl. Ah-ooooo!"

        "That _____ mean a thing!" said the cowboy.
                15
"Real coyotes have fur coats, _____ they? Look at
                                16
them. _____ all got fur."
        17

        Bill glanced around. "I _____ got any fur."
                                18
        "You _____ be here, _____ for
                19   20
sure," said the cowboy. "Come home with me."

        Bill said good-bye to his animal family. "I'll never forget you,"

he told them in coyote talk.

        And Pecos Bill climbed upon his pet mountain lion and

galloped off to a new life as the best cowboy the Texas prairie has

ever seen.

that's
she'd
they've
weren't
doesn't
isn't
wouldn't
wasn't
aren't
we're
you'd
don't
I'm
hadn't
haven't
didn't
shouldn't
let's
couldn't
they'll

★ Challenge Yourself ★

Challenge Words

it'd	should've
must've	there're

Write the two words that make up each Challenge
Word. Check a dictionary to see if you are right. Then
use separate paper to write sentences showing that you
understand the meaning of each Challenge Word.

21. There're some great storytellers in my family. _____

22. My grandfather **should've** written his stories down to help me remember
        them. _____

23. I **must've** been three years old when I first heard the story about the pet
        crocodile. _____

24. The story isn't true, but **it'd** make a great movie. _____

Name: Date:

Lesson 16

More Words with Short *u*

sponge

1. *o* Words
_____
_____
_____
_____
_____
_____
_____
_____
_____
_____
_____

2. *o-consonant-e* Words
_____
_____

3. *oo* Word
_____

wonderful
discover
among
blood
front
other
brother
money
cover
month
monkey
done
sponge
nothing
above
stomach
once
become
another
won

Say and Listen
Say each spelling word. Listen for the short *u* sound.

Think and Sort
Look at the letters in each word. Think about how short *u* is spelled. Spell each word aloud.

Short *u* can be shown as /ŭ/. How many spelling patterns for /ŭ/ do you see?

1. Write the sixteen spelling words that have the *o* pattern.

2. Write the three spelling words that have the *o-consonant-e* pattern.

3. Write the one spelling word that has the *oo* pattern.

Use the steps on page 4 to study words that are hard for you.

Spelling Patterns

o	**o-consonant-e**	**oo**
fr**o**nt	bec**o**m**e**	bl**oo**d

Spelling and Meaning

Antonyms Write the spelling word that is an antonym of each word below.

1. below _____

2. back _____

3. unfinished _____

4. lost _____

5. horrible _____

6. something _____

Clues Write the spelling word for each clue.

7. A girl is a sister, and a boy is this.

8. Food is digested in this body part.

9. This is one less than twice.

10. This word means "to grow to be."

11. Your heart pumps this through your body.

12. This can soak up water.

13. February is the shortest one.

14. This word means "in the company of."

15. This is a chimpanzee's cousin.

16. This word completes the phrase "some _____ time."

17. People use this to buy things.

18. This means "one more."

19. Do this to hide something.

_____
_____
_____
_____
_____
_____
_____
_____
_____
_____
_____
_____
_____

Word **Story** A **prefix** is one or more letters added to the beginning of a base word. A prefix changes the meaning of the base word and makes a new word. One of the spelling words contains the prefix *dis-* and means "to find out." Write the word.

20. _____

Family Tree: *cover* Think about how the *cover* words are alike in spelling and meaning. Then add another *cover* word to the tree.

covering

21.

discover   covers

cover

Name: _____   Date: _____

Spelling in Context

Use each spelling word once to complete the selection.

Monkeys

Millions of people visit zoos each year. Large crowds always seem to gather in _____ of the 1 _____ areas to watch these 2 funny, _____ animals at play. 3

There are many different types of monkeys, and they are all different sizes. Monkeys have warm _____. They also have 4 fur to _____ their body. Some 5 monkeys sleep in the daytime and live high _____ the ground in trees. 6

Most monkeys live in places that are warm throughout every _____ of the 7 year. These places must have trees and plenty of food. A large monkey needs a lot of food to fill its _____! 8

Monkeys live in groups. Sometimes the group is divided into families. Each family contains a father, a mother, and even a sister and _____. Monkeys watch 9 out for one _____. If one of the animals should _____ 10 11 danger, it will call out an alarm to the _____ monkeys. 12

Monkeys are very smart. They take in information like a _____ 13 soaking up water. When a monkey is taught how to do a new task, the monkey repeats it with few mistakes. Rhesus monkeys have even been used in spaceflights! Some scientists have _____ awards for work done with rhesus monkeys. 14

© Harcourt Achieve Inc. All rights reserved.

Even though monkeys are _____ the best-loved
₁₅
animals in the world, the number of monkeys grows smaller each
year. One reason is that they are losing their homes. Jungles that
_____ were large places for many monkeys to live
₁₆
are being cut down. Some monkeys are also killed for their fur,
which is worth a lot of _____. What is being
₁₇
_____ to stop the killing of monkeys? There are
₁₈
many laws in place to protect monkeys so that they do not
_____ extinct.
₁₉

     Many people feel it would be wrong to do _____
₂₀
to save the monkeys. What do you think?

wonderful
discover
among
blood
front
other
brother
money
cover
month
monkey
done
sponge
nothing
above
stomach
once
become
another
won

★ Challenge Yourself ★

Challenge Words

loveliest
hover
wondrous
undiscovered

What do you think each Challenge Word means? Check a
dictionary to see if you are right. Then use separate
paper to write sentences showing that you understand
the meaning of each Challenge Word.

21. The beautiful tulips made Ping's garden the
loveliest one in town.

22. We watched the hummingbird **hover** near the flowers.

23. Visiting the museum was a **wondrous** experience for Anita.

24. Although we know a great deal about oceans, many of their
secrets remain **undiscovered**.

Lesson 17

Words with /o͝o/

brook

1. *oo* Words
_____
_____
_____
_____
_____
_____
_____
_____

2. *u* Words
_____
_____
_____
_____
_____
_____

3. *ou* Words
_____
_____
_____
_____

4. *o* Words
_____
_____

wool
understood
cooked
should
stood
full
notebook
bush
brook
could
sugar
wooden
good-bye
pull
wolf
would
pudding
yours
during
woman

Say and Listen
Say each spelling word. Listen for the vowel sound you hear in *wool*.

Think and Sort
Look at the letters in each word. Think about how the vowel sound in *wool* is spelled. Spell each word aloud.

The vowel sound in wool can be shown as /o͝o/. How many spelling patterns for /o͝o/ do you see?

1. Write the eight spelling words that have the *oo* pattern.

2. Write the six spelling words that have the *u* pattern.

3. Write the four spelling words that have the *ou* pattern.

4. Write the two spelling words that have the *o* pattern.

Use the steps on page 4 to study words that are hard for you.

Spelling Patterns

oo	**u**	**ou**	**o**
w**oo**l	f**u**ll	c**ou**ld	w**o**lf

www.harcourtschoolsupply.com
© Harcourt Achieve Inc. All rights reserved.

Lesson 17: Words with /o͝o/
Core Skills Spelling 4, SV 9781419034084

Name: _____ Date: _____

Spelling and Meaning

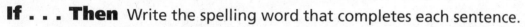

Synonyms Write the spelling word that is a synonym for each word below.

1. tug   _____

2. lady   _____

3. while   _____

4. stream   _____

5. stuffed   _____

6. shrub   _____

If . . . Then Write the spelling word that completes each sentence.

7. If you are cold, then put on a _____ sweater.

8. If you want dessert, then ask for cake or _____.

9. If you want to bake, then you may need _____ and flour.

10. If the meat is burnt, then it's been _____ too long.

11. If you need to write, then get a _____ and a pen.

12. If you hear a lone howl, then it might be a _____.

13. If it's not mine, then it may be _____.

14. If no one sat, then everyone _____.

15. If a bench is made from trees, then it's _____.

Rhymes Use spelling words to complete the following poem.

16. I meant that I was able when I said, "I _____."

17. I meant that I really ought to when I said, "I _____."

18. I meant that I planned to do it when I said, "I _____."

19. I said it very clearly to be sure you _____!

Word Story Long ago in England, the phrase "God be with you" was a common way of saying farewell. Over the years this phrase was shortened to "God be wy you." Even later it was shortened to "Godbwye." Write the spelling word it has become today.

20. _____

Family Tree: cook *Cooked* is a form of *cook*. Think about how the *cook* words are alike in spelling and meaning. Then add another *cook* word to the tree.

cooks

21. _____

cooked   uncooked

cook

© Harcourt Achieve Inc. All rights reserved.

Lesson 17: Words with /o͞o/
Core Skills Spelling 4, SV 9781419034084

Spelling in Context
Use each spelling word once to complete the story.

Mrs. Novik's Place

When I was a child, my favorite season was autumn. When the first cold autumn wind blew, my sister, Caroline, and I would _____ on our

_____ clothing and head for the woods. We _____
        2   3
walk through miles of oak trees, sometimes spotting a deer hiding behind a

_____. Late in the afternoon, we would often hear a
        4

_____ howling in the distance.
        5

A _____ bridge crossed a _____ by Claney
        6   7
Mountain. Just past the bridge _____ a lonely cabin. It belonged to
                                        8
Mrs. Novik. Most people around there thought that she was a strange old

_____. They said that children _____ stay away from her
        9   10
cabin. None of the adults _____ understand why Ma and Pa stood up
                                  11
for Mrs. Novik, but Caroline and I _____, especially after one October
                                            12
day in 1892.

Caroline and I brought Mrs. Novik some tasty _____ cookies that
                                                          13
Ma had baked. Mrs. Novik served us some delicious chocolate _____
                                                                      14
that she had _____. When Caroline and I were _____ of
                  15   16
the wonderful treat, I read Mrs. Novik a story I had written about her. "You are a fine

writer, Jonathan," she said when I finished. "I want to

give you something." She got up and came back with

an old _____. "This is my journal," she
        17
told me. "It tells the story of my life. Take it. It is now

_____."
        18

I sat by Mrs. Novik's fire all that afternoon,

reading her journal. From it I learned about her hard times _____ the
                                                                    19
Civil War. As I closed the book, a letter fell out:

Dear Mrs. Novik,

My husband is with us at last. Your food and care saved him. My family will never forget your kindness.

Mrs. Jonathan Walker

"Mrs. Jonathan Walker? That's Grandma!" I said. Then I remembered Grandma's stories about the people of the Underground Railroad and the lady who hid runaway slaves during the war. Now I knew that the lady who hid Grandpa was Mrs. Novik. Soon Caroline and I told Mrs. Novik _____ and headed home. I
20
couldn't wait to tell Ma and Pa what I had learned.

The cabin is gone now, and so is that old bridge. But sometimes even now, I hike out to Claney Mountain in the autumn. I think about Mrs. Novik and the great kindness she showed to my family.

wool
understood
cooked
should
stood
full
notebook
bush
brook
could
sugar
wooden
good-bye
pull
wolf
would
pudding
yours
during
woman

★ Challenge Yourself ★

Challenge Words

bookstore
misunderstood
rural
swoosh

Write the Challenge Word for each clue. Check a dictionary to see if you are right. Then use separate paper to write sentences showing that you understand the meaning of each Challenge Word.

21. This word describes fields of farms and open land.

_____

22. This is a rushing and swirling sound. _____

23. If writers do not write clearly, they might be this. _____

24. This building always has many stories. _____

Lesson 18

Words with /ōo/ or /yōo/

cougar

Say and Listen

Say each spelling word. Listen for the vowel sound you hear in *goose* and *beautiful*.

Think and Sort

The vowel sound in *goose* and *beautiful* can be shown as /ōo/. In *beautiful* and some other /ōo/ words, a *y* is pronounced before the /ōo/.

Look at the letters in each word. Think about how /ōo/ or /yōo/ is spelled. Spell each word aloud.

1. oo Words

_____
_____
_____
_____
_____
_____
_____

2. ew Words

_____
_____
_____

3. u Words

_____
_____

4. ou Words

_____
_____
_____
_____
_____

5. ui, o, eau Words

_____
_____
_____

goose
beautiful
cougar
route
balloon
too
soup
knew
group
two
grew
through
new
cartoon
truly
fruit
loose
shoot
truth
choose

1. Write the seven spelling words that have the *oo* pattern.

2. Write the three spelling words that have the *ew* pattern.

3. Write the two spelling words that have the *u* pattern.

4. Write the five spelling words that have the *ou* pattern.

5. Write the three spelling words that have the *ui*, *o*, or *eau* pattern.

Use the steps on page 4 to study words that are hard for you.

Spelling Patterns

oo	ew	u	ou
g**oo**se	n**ew**	tr**u**th	gr**ou**p

ui	o	eau	
fr**ui**t	tw**o**	b**eau**tiful	

Name: _____   Date: _____

Spelling and Meaning

Homophones Write the spelling word that is a homophone of each word below.

1. chute   _____
2. knew   _____
3. root   _____
4. threw   _____
5. two   _____

Analogies Write the spelling word that completes each analogy.

6. *Throw* is to *threw* as *know* is to _____.
7. *One* is to _____ as *A* is to *B*.
8. *Yes* is to *no* as *ugly* is to _____.
9. *Day* is to *night* as _____ is to *lie*.
10. *Bird* is to *flock* as *member* is to _____.
11. *Dirt* is to *flowerpot* as *air* is to _____.
12. *Light* is to *dark* as *tight* is to _____.
13. *Rabbit* is to *fur* as _____ is to *feather*.
14. *Apple* is to _____ as *spinach* is to *vegetable*.
15. *Afraid* is to *frightened* as *really* is to _____.
16. *Fork* is to *spaghetti* as *spoon* is to _____.
17. *Painter* is to *painting* as *cartoonist* is to _____.
18. *Smile* is to *grin* as _____ is to *pick*.
19. *Fly* is to *flew* as *grow* is to _____.

Word Story   One of the spelling words names an animal that is the same color as a deer. The word comes from the Tupi Indian word *suasuarana*. *Suasuarana* meant "false deer." The name became *couguar* in French. Write the word.

20. _____

Family Tree: *knew* *Knew* is a form of *know*. Think about how the *know* words are alike in spelling and meaning. Then add another *know* word to the tree.

knowledge

21.

knows   knew

know

Lesson 18: Words with /o͞o/ or /yo͞o/
Core Skills Spelling 4, SV 9781419034084

Spelling in Context

Use each spelling word once to complete the selection.

The Life of a Snow Goose

Have you ever seen a _____ of snow

geese flying across the sky? Like a well-trained dancer,

each _____ keeps its place in the flock

while flying. The flock often flies in the shape of a V. Now

that is a _____ sight!

In the spring, snow geese fly north to their nesting

grounds. When they arrive, they _____

nesting places. After a male and female choose a spot, the _____ of them

fight off any goose that comes _____ close. Then the mother lays her

eggs. The parents scare away enemies, such as the Arctic fox. When defending its nest, a

snow goose can be as fierce as a snarling _____.

After the eggs hatch, the parents teach the babies to find food and to fly. Snow geese

keep their little ones in a group. They do not let them run _____. At

night the whole family sleeps together. Snow geese are _____ good

parents!

In the fall the snow geese fly south. When they get hungry, they land in a field. They

eat seeds, tender green plants, and _____ such as cranberries.

For hundreds of years, flocks of geese followed the same _____

every year. Somehow they always _____ how to find the same path.

They could fly through fog as thick as pea _____ without losing their

way! Flocks often take a _____ route today. This route passes

_____ areas where there are grain farms. The geese eat the grains to

fatten up for the winter.

Name: _____   Date: _____

It is hard for the grain farmers to watch the crops that they
_____ be eaten by geese. That is why they try to scare
      16
the geese away. Some farmers tie a brightly colored helium
_____ to each fence post. Other farmers
      17
_____ firecrackers into the air.
      18
    The _____ on this page is a joke, but it tells the
             19
_____ about snow geese. They do not like freezing
      20
weather, so they spend the winter in a warm place. At winter's end,
they return to their nesting grounds to start new families.

goose
beautiful
cougar
route
balloon
too
soup
knew
group
two
grew
through
new
cartoon
truly
fruit
loose
shoot
truth
choose

Are you cold, dear?

Yes! Just look at my goosebumps!

★ Challenge Yourself ★

Use a dictionary to answer the questions. Then use separate paper to write sentences showing that you understand the meaning of each Challenge Word.

Challenge Words

accuse

boost

contribute

coupon

21. Would a small child need a **boost** to climb onto a horse? _____

22. Do you pay more money for an item at the grocery store when you use a **coupon**? _____

23. If you **accuse** someone of stealing, are you saying he or she did something wrong? _____

24. Do people **contribute** cans and boxes of food to help feed others? _____

Lesson 19

Words with /ou/

tower

1. *ou* Words

_____
_____
_____
_____
_____
_____
_____
_____
_____
_____

2. *ow* Words

_____
_____
_____
_____
_____
_____
_____
_____
_____
_____

loud
counter
somehow
hours
powerful
sour
crowd
growl
cloud
towel
ours
south
crowded
mouth
vowel
shower
crown
tower
noun
proud

Say and Listen

Say each spelling word. Listen for the vowel sound you hear in *loud*.

Think and Sort

Look at the letters in each word. Think about how the vowel sound in *loud* is spelled. Spell each word aloud.

The vowel sound in *loud* can be shown as /ou/. How many spelling patterns for /ou/ do you see?

1. Write the ten spelling words that have the *ou* pattern.

2. Write the ten spelling words that have the *ow* pattern.

Use the steps on page 4 to study words that are hard for you.

Spelling Patterns

ou	ow
loud	cr**ow**n

www.harcourtschoolsupply.com
© Harcourt Achieve Inc. All rights reserved.

Lesson 19: Words with /ou/
Core Skills Spelling 4, SV 9781419034084

Name: _____   Date: _____

Spelling and Meaning

Classifying Write the spelling word that belongs in each group.

1. robe, throne, _____
2. seconds, minutes, _____
3. eye, nose, _____
4. group, bunch, _____
5. sweet, salty, _____
6. noisy, booming, _____
7. drizzle, sprinkle, _____
8. bark, snarl, _____
9. east, north, _____
10. mighty, strong, _____
11. yours, theirs, _____
12. full, packed, _____

Partner Words Complete each sentence by writing the spelling word that goes with the underlined word.

13. Do you want to sit in a <u>booth</u> or at the _____?
14. <u>Someone</u> somewhere must rescue the princess _____.
15. The castle had a _____ and a <u>moat</u>.
16. I'll get you a _____ and a <u>washcloth</u>.
17. <u>Rain</u> will soon fall from that dark _____.
18. Jamal was <u>pleased</u> with and _____ of his sister's work.
19. You can choose a _____ or a <u>consonant</u>.

Word **Story**   One of the spelling words names a part of speech. It comes from the Latin word *nomen,* meaning "name." Write the word.

20. _____

Family Tree: *powerful* *Powerful* is a form of *power*. Think about how the *power* words are alike in spelling and meaning. Then add another *power* word to the tree.

powered

21. _____

powerless   powerful

power

© Harcourt Achieve Inc. All rights reserved.
Lesson 19: Words with /ou/
Core Skills Spelling 4, SV 9781419034084

Name: _____   Date: _____

Spelling in Context

Use each spelling word once to complete the selection.

An Ancient Code

Did you know that writing came from art? People had been drawing pictures
for many years. As time passed, they _____ got the idea of using
                                              1
pictures to stand for words. In picture writing, each picture stands for a verb or a
_____. For example, a picture of a _____ might stand for
         2   3
king. A _____ of raindrops falling from a _____ might
                    4   5
stand for *rain*. A _____ or lips might be used for *talk* or *say*. Early
                              6
Egyptians used picture writing. They drew each picture very carefully. It took them many
_____ to write a message.
          7
The writing of the ancient Egyptians was very different from _____.
                                                                              8
Experts have learned that the writing contained more than just pictures. There were also
symbols for the sounds of consonants, such as *g* and *t*. However, there were no symbols for
any of the _____ sounds. No one knows how the words sounded when
                      9
they were spoken out _____. A word with only consonants would
                                  10
probably sound like an animal _____!
                                            11
Picture writing has been found in both the north and the _____ of
                                                                              12
Egypt. The writings show how _____ Egyptians were of their rulers and
                                          13

their gods. Writing covered the walls of temples. Tales of strong and

_____ **14** rulers were carved on obelisks. An obelisk is a

tall, thin _____ **15** .

Picture writing has also been found on mummies and treasures in

many Egyptian tombs. As workers wrapped a mummy, they hid picture

messages. First workers laid the body on a long wooden table or

_____ **16** to wash it. Then they used a

_____ **17** to rub on perfumed oil. That kept the body

from smelling _____ **18** . Last they wrapped the body in

cloth strips. Between the layers of cloth, they tucked notes in picture

writing. The notes warned away bad spirits. Then a large

_____ **19** of mourners carried the body to the tomb.

Others carried food, clothing, and jewels. They buried these things

with their loved one. A tomb could be very _____ **20** !

After modern scientists found the tombs, they spent years studying

the picture writing there. The writing reveals much about ancient

Egyptian life. As scientists have learned to decode the writing, they

have unlocked a door to the past.

loud
counter
somehow
hours
powerful
sour
crowd
growl
cloud
towel
ours
south
crowded
mouth
vowel
shower
crown
tower
noun
proud

★ Challenge Yourself ★

Challenge Words

drowsy
counselor
encounter
blouse

Write the Challenge Word for each clue. Check a dictionary to see if you are right. Then use separate paper to write sentences showing that you understand the meaning of each Challenge Word.

21. This is a person you go to for advice.

_____

22. Seeing a friend at a store and stopping to say hello is an example of this. _____

23. A girl wears this piece of clothing with pants or a skirt. _____

24. It's how you feel early in the morning after staying up too late.

_____

Lesson 20
Words with -ed or -ing

swimming

1. No Change to Base Word

_____
_____
_____

2. Final e Dropped

_____
_____
_____
_____
_____
_____
_____
_____
_____
_____

3. Final Consonant Doubled

_____
_____
_____

4. Final y Changed to i

_____
_____
_____
_____

swimming
asked
hoping
changed
pleased
beginning
caused
traded
closing
invited
tasted
jogging
studied
copied
dried
saving
cried
trying
carrying
writing

Say and Listen
Say the spelling words. Listen for the -ed and -ing endings.

Think and Sort
A word from which other words are formed is called a **base word.** The spelling of some base words changes when -ed or -ing is added.

Look at the base word and the ending in each spelling word. Spell each word aloud.

1. Write the three spelling words that have no change to the base word.

2. Write the ten spelling words formed by dropping the final e before -ed or -ing is added.

3. Write the three spelling words formed by doubling the final consonant before -ing is added.

4. Write the four spelling words formed by changing the final y to i before -ed is added.

Use the steps on page 4 to study words that are hard for you.

Spelling Patterns

No Change to Base Word	Final e Dropped
asked	**hop**ing
Final Consonant Doubled	**Final y Changed to i**
swim**m**ing	stud**i**ed

Name: _____   Date: _____

Spelling and Meaning

Making Connections Write the spelling word
that goes with each person.

1. a mail carrier   _____
2. a lifeguard   _____
3. a runner   _____
4. a cook   _____
5. an author   _____
6. a baby   _____
7. a student   _____

If . . . Then Write the spelling word that completes each sentence.

8. If Ramon exchanged baseball cards, then he _____ them.
9. If Carlos is putting money in a bank, then he's _____ it.
10. If Amad wishes for a bicycle, then he's _____ for one.
11. If Mr. Bina is shutting the door, then he's _____ it.
12. If Tyler begged for help, then he _____ for it.
13. If Dad liked the work, then he was _____ with it.
14. If Sarah imitated the star's hairdo, then she _____ it.
15. If Troy asked his friends to a party, then he _____ them.
16. If the sun is coming up, then it is _____ to be seen.
17. If Sam wiped away his tears, then he _____ them.
18. If Lamont is not the same, then he has _____.
19. If heavy rain loosened the mud, then it _____ a mudslide.

Word Story   One of the
spelling words comes from the Old
French word *trier*. *Trier* meant "to pick
out." The spelling word has several
meanings—"to sample," "to test," or
"to attempt." Write the *-ing* form of
this word.

20. _____

Family Tree: *pleased* *Pleased* is a
form of *please*. Think about how the *please*
words are alike in spelling and meaning.
Then add another *please* word to the tree.

pleased

21. _____

pleasure   pleases

please

© Harcourt Achieve Inc. All rights reserved.
Lesson 20: Words with *-ed* or *-ing*
Core Skills Spelling 4, SV 9781419034084

Spelling in Context

Use each spelling word once to complete the selection.

J.J. Returns to the Sea

A mother whale was on her way south when something unexpected happened. The baby she was _____ **1** was born early! The baby whale, or calf, had trouble _____ **2** in the cold ocean water. The calf lost her way.

One day the calf swam near a California beach. People who were walking and _____ **3** along the shore saw that the young whale was in trouble. They _____ **4** others to help. Soon police and animal experts were _____ **5** to get the baby to shore. Finally, they got the whale onto a truck. Then they took her to a marine park. This move _____ **6** everyone.

Caretakers at the park named the baby whale J.J. The animal doctors there _____ **7** J.J. The young whale was constantly _____ **8** her eyes. She could not hold herself steady. What had _____ **9** these problems? J.J. was only one week old and hadn't eaten in days!

The doctors mixed cream, fish, and water for her. They hoped the mix _____ **10** like the milk J.J. was used to. In the _____ **11**, J.J.'s caretakers poured her food down a tube to her stomach. Soon, however, the calf could drink for herself.

Many people were interested in J.J.s recovery. Caretakers began _____ **12** messages on special Web site. They wanted to let J.J.'s fans know how she was doing.

During J.J.'s first month at the park, she _____ **13** a lot. J.J. gained 900 pounds! Caretakers _____ **14** her small pool for a roomier one.

84

_____ that J. J. would learn to communicate, they then
      15

began playing whale songs for her. J. J. listened to the recordings and

_____ the sounds she heard.
      16

    Soon it was time for J. J. to go back to the sea. Her caretakers were

_____ to ride with J. J. in the truck. They sprayed J. J.
      17

with water often to keep her skin from becoming

_____ out.
      18

    At last J. J. was lowered into the sea. As her caretakers said

good-bye, some _____. They had played a big part in
                          19

_____ J. J.'s life and would miss her. Everyone knew,
      20

however, that J. J. was finally back where she belonged!

swimming
asked
hoping
changed
pleased
beginning
caused
traded
closing
invited
tasted
jogging
studied
copied
dried
saving
cried
trying
carrying
writing

★ Challenge Yourself ★

Challenge Words

hustled

importing

overlapping

fortified

What do you think each Challenge Word means? Check a dictionary to see if you are right. Then use separate paper to write sentences showing that you understand the meaning of each Challenge Word.

21. Because I overslept, I **hustled** to meet the school bus on time.

22. The United States is **importing** oil from several countries.

23. Be sure the edges of the tent are **overlapping** so that rain can't get in.

24. During the flood, we **fortified** the banks of the river with sandbags.

Lesson 21

Words with /oi/

soil

1. *oy* Words

_____
_____
_____
_____
_____
_____

2. *oi* Words

_____
_____
_____
_____
_____
_____
_____
_____
_____

coin
moisture
enjoy
spoil
destroy
employ
point
employer
loyal
royal
poison
soil
join
voyage
loyalty
avoid
voice
noise
soybean
choice

Say and Listen

Say each spelling word. Listen for the vowel sound you hear in *coin*.

Think and Sort

Look at the letters in each word. Think about how the vowel sound in *coin* is spelled. Spell each word aloud.

The vowel sound in *coin* can be shown as /oi/. How many spelling patterns for /oi/ do you see?

1. Write the nine spelling words that have the *oy* pattern.

2. Write the eleven spelling words that have the *oi* pattern.

Use the steps on page 4 to study words that are hard for you.

Spelling Patterns

oy	oi
enj**oy**	c**oi**n

Spelling and Meaning

Clues Write the spelling word for each clue.

1. A ship can take you on this. _____
2. This is very harmful to living things. _____
3. You can dig in this. _____
4. Dogs are this to their masters. _____
5. When you can decide between two things, you have this. _____
6. You put this in a parking meter. _____
7. The end of an arrow has this. _____
8. An opera singer uses this. _____
9. People work for this person. _____
10. This plant has nutritious seeds. _____
11. Good friends share this with each other. _____
12. Water adds this to the air. _____

Antonyms Complete each sentence by writing the spelling word that is an antonym of the underlined word.

13. They had to _____ the old house and build a new one.
14. We can separate or _____ these two wires.
15. Will the rain improve or _____ the crops?
16. Do you dislike your dancing lessons or _____ them?
17. Hector needs silence in order to study, not _____.
18. Will the store fire its workers and _____ new ones?
19. I will meet Laura at the store early and _____ the crowd.

Word Story Three English words mean "fit for a king." *Kingly* is from the Old English word *king*. *Regal* comes from the Latin word *rex*. One of the spelling words comes from the French word *roi*. Write the word.

20. _____

Family Tree: *point* Think about how the *point* words are alike in spelling and meaning. Then add another *point* word to the tree.

- pointer
- 21. _____
- pointed
- pointless
- **point**

Spelling in Context

Use each spelling word once to complete the selection.

Treasure from China

During the 1200s and 1300s, many travelers visited China. One of them was the explorer Marco Polo. After a very long _____ by sea and land, Polo

1
arrived in China in 1274. There he earned the trust of the ruler, Kublai Khan. Polo worked in China's government and was _____ to Kublai Khan. In return

2
Khan rewarded Polo's service and _____ with many gifts. In 1292 Marco

3
Polo thanked his generous _____ and returned to Italy with spices, jade,

4
silk, and stories.

Polo told other people about the many treasures he saw in China. In a
_____ loud and clear, he described the beauty and loud

5
_____ of fireworks. He told how paper money was used instead of a

6
single gold or silver _____. But neither Polo nor any of the other visitors

7
to China talked about the small green bean that grew in China's fields—the
_____ . That small green bean became a great world treasure.

8
Soybeans did not reach Europe until the 1700s. They were grown in special gardens in France. They were even grown in the English king's _____ gardens.

9
Soon the Chinese beans were brought to North America. At that _____

10
an important industry began.

Scientists in the United States studied about 10,000 kinds of soybeans. Farmers could decide which one was the best _____ for their part of the country. Some kinds needed lots of rain. Others needed less _____.

Soybeans could grow in almost any kind of dirt. They did best, however, in rich, well-drained _____. The plants were easy to keep healthy, too. A plant disease would almost never _____ the whole crop. Scientists later developed soybean plants that did not attract insects. In fact, bugs would _____ the new plants. Since most bugs stayed away, farmers could use less _____.

Today soybean farms _____ thousands of workers. Soybeans are used to make everything from paint to pet food. They are used in many foods that people eat and _____ every day, such as cereal and ice cream.

As countries _____ together to fight world hunger, soybeans are their best weapon. Soybeans have more protein than meat. They don't _____ or rot. Soybeans cost less than meat, too! Of all the treasures China has given the world, the soybean may just be the most important.

Word list (spiral notepad):

coin
moisture
enjoy
spoil
destroy
employ
point
employer
loyal
royal
poison
soil
join
voyage
loyalty
avoid
voice
noise
soybean
choice

★ Challenge Yourself ★

Challenge Words

appoint	poise
pointless	toil

Write the Challenge Word for each clue. Check a dictionary to see if you are right. Then use separate paper to write sentences showing that you understand the meaning of each Challenge Word.

21. People who have this are calm under pressure. _____
22. To pull weeds all day in the hot sun is to do this. _____
23. This word tells what it is like to try to teach a fish to talk. _____
24. This is one way a teacher can get a helper. _____

Lesson 22
Words with /ô/

autumn

1. *au* Words
_____
_____
_____
_____
_____
_____

2. *o* Words
_____
_____
_____
_____
_____
_____
_____

3. *augh* Words
_____
_____
_____

4. *ough* Words
_____
_____
_____

5. *a* Word
_____

pause
already
brought
strong
taught
caught
cause
because
wrong
coffee
bought
thought
author
applaud
autumn
daughter
gone
offer
often
office

Say and Listen
Say each spelling word. Listen for the vowel sound you hear in *pause*.

Think and Sort
Look at the letters in each word. Think about how the vowel sound in *pause* is spelled. Spell each word aloud.

The vowel sound in pause can be shown as /ô/. How many spelling patterns for /ô/ do you see?

1. Write the six spelling words that have the *au* pattern.

2. Write the seven spelling words that have the *o* pattern.

3. Write the three spelling words that have the *augh* pattern.

4. Write the three spelling words that have the *ough* pattern.

5. Write the one spelling word that has the *a* pattern.

Use the steps on page 4 to study words that are hard for you.

Spelling Patterns

au	**o**	**augh**	**ough**	**a**
p**au**se	**strong**	t**augh**t	b**ough**t	**a**lready

www.harcourtschoolsupply.com
© Harcourt Achieve Inc. All rights reserved.

Lesson 22: Words with /ô/
Core Skills Spelling 4, SV 9781419034084

Spelling and Meaning

Classifying Write the spelling word that belongs in each group.

1. instructed, showed, _____
2. clap, cheer, _____
3. powerful, mighty, _____
4. incorrect, mistaken, _____
5. purchased, paid, _____
6. believed, supposed, _____
7. spring, summer, _____
8. captured, grabbed, _____
9. writer, creator, _____
10. stop, rest, _____
11. parent, son, _____
12. delivered, carried, _____
13. give, present, _____

If . . . Then Write the spelling word that completes each sentence.

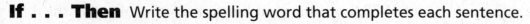

14. If Mary jogs four days a week, then she does it _____.
15. If Kara's cat is not here, then it is _____.
16. If Jon is finished with his work, then he's _____ done.
17. If Mom has a special room for working, then she has an _____.
18. If James wins many races, then it's _____ he's a fast runner.
19. If a storm can bend trees, then it might _____ them to fall.

Word Story One spelling word names a bean and the drink made from the bean. Some people think the word comes from the Arabic word *qahwah*, meaning "a strong drink." Write the word.

20. _____

Family Tree: *thought* Think about how the *thought* words are alike in spelling and meaning. Then add another *thought* word to the tree.

thoughtfulness

21. _____

rethought   thoughtful

thought

Spelling in Context

Use each spelling word once to complete the selection.

Lorraine Hansberry

Lorraine Hansberry was born in Chicago, Illinois, on May 19, 1930. She was the

youngest _____ of Carl and Nannie Hansberry. By the age of 13,
                    1

Lorraine _____ knew she wanted a job in the theater.
                  2

After high school Lorraine went to college. There she learned about great writers

and was _____ how to put on plays. Soon she began writing her own
                3

plays and moved to New York City. At first she wasn't able to earn money as an

_____. She took odd jobs. She was a clerk in an _____.
              4   5

Then she waited on tables in a _____ shop, where people
                                                          6

_____ breakfast and lunch.
            7

In the _____ of 1957, Lorraine read her friends part of a play she'd
              8

written. When she finished, they began to _____. Lorraine's friends took
                                                                  9

the play to some theater people, who agreed to put it on. The play was called *A Raisin in*

the Sun.

Lorraine had very _____ feelings about equal rights. She
                              10

_____ it was _____ to judge people because of their
          11   12

race. The actors in her play talked about those ideas. People were moved

_____ of the way the feelings of African Americans were explained on
          13

the stage.

A Raisin in the Sun became a hit and _____ Lorraine fame and
                                                            14

awards. She became the youngest woman and

the first African American woman to receive a

major prize for a play. Soon a film company

made her an _____ to make a
                    15

movie of her play.

92

Name: _____ Date: _____

Lorraine then became _____ up in the civil
16
rights movement. Because it was a _____ she believed
17
in, she started writing a book about it. But she became ill and had to
_____ in her work.
18
In January 1965 Lorraine Hansberry died. Even though she is
_____, her work still remains. The movie *A Raisin in*
19
the Sun is _____ shown on television. A few years ago,
20
Lorraine's friends produced a play called *To Be Young, Gifted, and Black*
about her life.

pause
already
brought
strong
taught
caught
cause
because
wrong
coffee
bought
thought
author
applaud
autumn
daughter
gone
offer
often
office

★ Challenge Yourself ★

Challenge Words

| auction | audio |
| precaution | offerings |

Use a dictionary to answer these questions. Then use
separate paper to write sentences showing that you
understand the meaning of each Challenge Word.

21. Does **audio** equipment help people see? _____
22. Can people buy things at an **auction**? _____
23. If you give cans of food to help homeless people, are the cans
of food your **offerings**? _____
24. Is locking the door a **precaution** against getting sick? _____

Lesson 23
More Words with /ô/

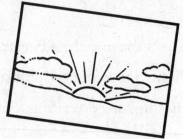

dawn

1. *aw* Words

_____
_____
_____
_____
_____

2. *a* Words

_____
_____
_____
_____

3. *o* Words

_____
_____
_____
_____
_____
_____
_____
_____
_____
_____
_____

lawn
toward
straw
morning
score
north
water
explore
dawn
crawl
quart
warm
before
shore
chorus
yawn
important
orbit
report
popcorn

Say and Listen
Say each spelling word. Listen for the vowel sound you hear in *lawn*.

Think and Sort
Look at the letters in each word. Think about how the vowel sound in *lawn* is spelled. Spell each word aloud.

The vowel sound in *lawn* can be shown as /ô/. How many spelling patterns for /ô/ do you see?

1. Write the five spelling words that have the *aw* pattern.

2. Write the four spelling words that have the *a* pattern.

3. Write the eleven spelling words that have the *o* pattern.

Use the steps on page 4 to study words that are hard for you.

Spelling Patterns

aw	a	o
lawn	w**a**ter	n**or**th

www.harcourtschoolsupply.com
© Harcourt Achieve Inc. All rights reserved.

Lesson 23: More Words with /ô/
Core Skills Spelling 4, SV 9781419034084

Spelling and Meaning

Definitions Write the spelling word for each definition. Use a dictionary if you need to.

1. a snack food made from heating corn _____
2. ground that is covered with grass _____
3. dried stalks of grain used for padding _____
4. having great worth or value _____
5. going in the direction of something _____
6. to open the mouth and take in air when tired _____
7. the path of one heavenly body around another _____
8. the number of points made by a player or team _____
9. organized oral or written information _____
10. the first appearance of daylight _____

Analogies Write the spelling word that completes each analogy.

11. *Evening* is to _____ as *night* is to *day*.
12. *After* is to _____ as *up* is to *down*.
13. *South* is to _____ as *east* is to *west*.
14. *Players* are to *team* as *singers* are to _____.
15. *Find* is to *discover* as *search* is to _____.
16. *Creep* is to _____ as *walk* is to *stroll*.
17. *Dry* is to *wet* as *cool* is to _____.
18. *Pint* is to _____ as *foot* is to *yard*.
19. *Desert* is to *sand* as *lake* is to _____.

Word **Story**   One spelling word comes from the Old English word *sceran*. *Sceran* meant "to cut." The spelling word means "land at the edge of a sea or lake." Write the word.

20. _____

Family Tree: *explore* Think about how the *explore* words are alike in spelling and meaning. Then add another *explore* word to the tree.

exploratory

21. _____

explored   exploring

explore

Name: _____   Date: _____

Spelling in Context

Use each spelling word once to complete the story.

Mysteries for the Moonship

One _____ Mr. Goodkind asked his students to go on a scavenger
                    1
hunt. He divided the class into teams. Each team decided on a name for itself. Zachary,
Katy, Mark, and Amanda chose Moonship as their team name. Then Mr. Goodkind gave
each team a list of things to find. The Moonship team began to groan. Their list was
hidden in three riddles. Mark read the first riddle:

> Let the pan go from _____ to hot,
>   **2**
> And into _____ I am shot.
>   **3**
> Sputter, sputter, pour on the butter!

"Let's go!" Zachary said. "Maybe the answer will pop into our heads. Pop . . .

_____!"
   4

"Popcorn's the answer!" the team shouted.

Moonship headed _____ Mark's house to get some popcorn. They
                        5
found a _____ of milk and drank it. Then Mark's dad helped them pop
              6
some popcorn. They washed the milk carton with _____ and put the
                                                        7
popcorn in. The second riddle was harder:

> From _____ to dark I nibble and _____.
>   **8**   **9**
> My soft fuzzy body is low and small.
> When the time comes, I spin a soft wrap.
> I _____ and curl up inside for a nap.
>   **10**
> I wake up and am not what I was before.
> I've beautiful wings and the sky to _____
>   **11**

"A baby takes a nap and crawls," said Mark. "Hey, Zachary! Stop eating our popcorn.

This is _____. Think!"
            12

"I am thinking about how good this popcorn would taste if it had some butter on it.

Butter . . . butterfly!" Zachary exclaimed.

© Harcourt Achieve Inc. All rights reserved.
Lesson 23: More Words with /ô/
Core Skills Spelling 4, SV 9781419034084

"No. But caterpillar is the answer!" said Amanda.

The Moonship team searched until they found a caterpillar near

the _____ of the pond at the city park. From there
                    13

they headed _____ to Katy's house.
                        14

Katy read the next riddle:

> In spring I rise, damp and green.
>
> In a place like a _____ is where I am seen.
>   15
> Yet soon I'm a basket, I'm a hat.
>
> I'm a broom, I'm a welcome mat.
>
> Scarecrows and haystacks are made from me.
>
> Burning matches I hate to see.

"_____!" the Moonship team sang out in
            16

_____ as they grabbed a broom from the kitchen.
        17

With the straw broom, caterpillar, and popcorn, they raced back to

school. Soon they arrived at their classroom to _____
                                                        18

to Mr. Goodkind.

"Well, Moonship," Mr. Goodkind said, "you got here

_____ the others. Your team will get a perfect
        19

_____! It looks like the Moonship made the first
        20

landing!"

Spelling Words
lawn
toward
straw
morning
score
north
water
explore
dawn
crawl
quart
warm
before
shore
chorus
yawn
important
orbit
report
popcorn

★ Challenge Yourself ★

Challenge Words

adorn	awesome
hoard	torture

What do you think each Challenge Word means? Check a dictionary to see if you are right. Then use separate paper to write sentences showing that you understand the meaning of each Challenge Word.

21. Jasper spends his allowance, but Kendra likes to **hoard** hers.
22. The view from the mountain was an **awesome** sight.
23. We decided to **adorn** the class float with ribbons and flowers.
24. It was **torture** to hike five miles in the hot sun.

Lesson 24

Words with /är/ or /âr/

marbles

Spelling Word List

1. /är/ Words
_____
_____
_____
_____
_____
_____
_____
_____

2. /âr/ Words
_____
_____
_____
_____
_____
_____
_____
_____
_____
_____
_____
_____

sharp
share
they're
marbles
their
where
smart
large
heart
careful
square
there
stairs
fair
air
fare
stares
scarf
apart
alarm

Say and Listen

The spelling words for this lesson contain the /är/ and /âr/ sounds that you hear in *sharp* and *share*. Say the spelling words. Listen for the /är/ and /âr/ sounds.

Think and Sort

Look at the letters in each word. Think about how the /är/ or /âr/ sounds are spelled. Spell each word aloud. How many spelling patterns for /är/ and /âr/ do you see?

1. The /är/ sounds can be spelled *ar* or *ear*. Write the eight /är/ spelling words. Underline the letters that spell /är/ in each word.

2. The /âr/ sounds can be spelled *are*, *air*, *ere*, *eir*, or *ey're*. Write the twelve /âr/ spelling words. Underline the letters that spell /âr/ in each word.

Use the steps on page 4 to study words that are hard for you.

Spelling Patterns

/är/	**ar** sh**ar**p	**ear** h**ear**t		
/âr/	**are** sh**are**	**air** f**air**	**ere** th**ere**	**eir** th**eir**	**ey're** th**ey're**

Name: _____ Date: _____

Spelling and Meaning

Classifying Write the spelling word that belongs in each group.

1. wind, breeze, _____
2. thorny, pointed, _____
3. bell, siren, _____
4. hat, gloves, _____
5. bright, clever, _____
6. big, huge, _____
7. separated, in pieces, _____
8. slow, watchful, _____
9. triangle, rectangle, _____
10. give, divide, _____
11. jacks, checkers, _____
12. who, what, _____

Homophones Complete each sentence with the spelling word that is a homophone of the underlined word.

13. Steven and Jake left _____ shoes over there.
14. The high fare for the plane trip is not _____.
15. Elena stares at the seven flights of _____.
16. The bus _____ to the fair was cheap.
17. They're waiting over _____ by the bench.
18. Today _____ bringing their projects to school.
19. Jess _____ at the ball as it bounces down the stairs.

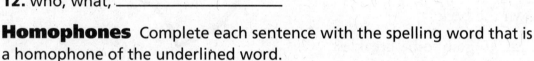

Word Story   The phrase "raining cats and dogs" is an **idiom**. The meanings of the words in an idiom don't add up to the meaning of the idiom. Write the spelling word that completes the following idiom.

I know that song by _____.

20. _____

Family Tree: _fair_ Think about how the _fair_ words are alike in spelling and meaning. Then add another _fair_ word to the tree.

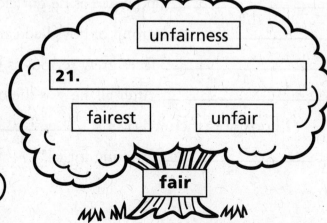

unfairness

21.

fairest   unfair

fair

© Harcourt Achieve Inc. All rights reserved.
Lesson 24: Words with /är/ or /âr/
Core Skills Spelling 4, SV 9781419034084

Spelling in Context

Use each spelling word once to complete the story.

The Marble Contest

Charlie woke at once when his

_____ went off. It was the
    1

morning of the marble contest. He reached

under his bed for his _____
                            2

and carefully placed his lucky one in a box.

Then he wrapped a big handful of them in

an old red _____, dressed
                3

quickly, and ran down the back

_____ to grab some breakfast.
        4

"Got everything you need?" his mother asked.

"You bet, Ma. I've got all of them ready to go. My lucky one is packed in a box.

Can't take a chance on losing that one!"

"Oh, Charlie! You're a _____ boy. You know that skill wins a game,
                              5

not luck," his mother said.

Charlie ate his toast and eggs and gathered his belongings. He was

_____ not to drop the small _____ box that held his
        6   7

lucky marble.

The crisp autumn _____ hummed with excitement, and Charlie's
                        8

_____ pounded as he got closer to the center of town. A very
        9

_____ group of boys had gathered in the village square.
        10

_____ faces grew serious as Charlie came near. He met their
        11

_____. After all, he was the champion!
        12

"Look at that crowd over _____," his friend Jess shouted.
                                13

"_____ waiting for us."
        14

The boys gathered around a circle in the dirt and soon were shooting marbles with quick, _____ flicks of their
15
fingers. When the marbles were knocked _____, laughs
16
and shouts went through the group.

As the day wore on, players were eliminated. Charlie and Jess were alone around the circle. Those who lost stayed to
_____ the thrill of the last match. Charlie pulled out
17
the box to place his lucky marble beside him.

"_____ is my tiger's-eye marble? Hold on! This
18
isn't _____! I must have left it at home!" he said. But
19
Jess and all of the boys wanted the game to go on.

"How could I have done this?" Charlie wondered. "OK, Ma. Now let's see what skill can do!" He aimed a marble at the center and closed his eyes. The marbles clicked, and a cheer rose from the crowd.

"The winner and still champion, Charlie Coleman!"

Charlie's prize was his _____ to the statewide
20
marble contest in St. Louis. Charlie grinned and looked at Jess. "I'll take my tiger's-eye marble to St. Louis," he said. "But who needs a lucky marble when you've got skill?"

sharp
share
they're
marbles
their
where
smart
large
heart
careful
square
there
stairs
fair
air
fare
stares
scarf
apart
alarm

★ Challenge Yourself ★

Challenge Words

collage	airborne
regardless	varnish

What do you think each Challenge Word means? Check a dictionary to see if you are right. Then use separate paper to write sentences showing that you understand the meaning of each Challenge Word.

21. We used string, colored paper, and buttons to make a **collage** to hang on the wall.
22. I could not see the **airborne** dust, but it made me sneeze.
24. The picnic will be held today, **regardless** of the weather.
25. The coat of **varnish** made the desk shine as if it were new.

Name: _____   Date: _____

Lesson 25
Plural and Possessive Words

sheep

1. Plural Nouns

_____
_____
_____
_____
_____
_____
_____
_____
_____
_____

2. Possessive Nouns

_____
_____
_____
_____
_____
_____
_____
_____

children
men
shelves
man's
cloud's
women
feet
woman's
women's
child's
teeth
children's
sheep
oxen
mice
geese
wife's
knives
wives
men's

Say and Listen
Say each spelling word. Listen to the sounds in each word.

Think and Sort
Some of the spelling words are **plural nouns**. They name more than one person, place, or thing. The usual way to form the plural of a noun is to add -s or -es. The plural nouns in this lesson are not formed in that way. They are called **irregular plurals**.

The other spelling words show ownership. They are called **possessive nouns**. How do all of these words end?

Look at each spelling word. Spell each word aloud.

1. Write the twelve spelling words that are plural nouns.

2. Write the eight spelling words that are possessive nouns.

Use the steps on page 4 to study words that are hard for you.

Spelling Patterns

Plurals		
m**en**	child**ren**	wi**ves**

Possessives		
man**'s**	child**'s**	wife**'s**
men**'s**	children**'s**	

www.harcourtschoolsupply.com
© Harcourt Achieve Inc. All rights reserved.

Lesson 25: Plural and Possessive Words
Core Skills Spelling 4, SV 9781419034084

Spelling and Meaning

Analogies Write the spelling word that completes each analogy.

1. *Horses* are to *hay* as _____ are to *cheese*.
2. *Drawers* are to *dressers* as _____ are to *bookcases*.
3. *Alligators* are to *reptiles* as _____ are to *birds*.
4. *Kittens* are to *cats* as *lambs* are to _____.
5. *Lawn mowers* are to *grass* as _____ are to *food*.
6. *Fingers* are to *hands* as *toes* are to _____.
7. *Floors* are to *mop* as _____ are to *brush*.
8. *Mothers* are to *women* as *fathers* are to _____.
9. *Child* is to *children* as *ox* is to _____.
10. *Gentlemen* are to *men* as *ladies* are to _____.
11. *Ducklings* are to *ducks* as _____ are to *humans*.

Trading Places Write the possessive word that can be used instead of the underlined words.

12. the shoes belonging to the man   the _____ shoes
13. the toy belonging to the child   the _____ toy
14. the parents of the wife   the _____ parents
15. the shape of the cloud   the _____ shape
16. the dresses belonging to the women   the _____ dresses
17. the books belonging to the children   the _____ books
18. the hands of the men   the _____ hands
19. the face of the woman   the _____ face

Word **Story** One spelling word comes from the Old English word *wif*. Long ago *wif* simply meant "a woman." Today the spelling word means "married women." Write the word.

20. _____

Family Tree: *children* *Children* is a form of *child*. Think about how the *child* words are alike in spelling and meaning. Then add another *child* word to the tree.

childless

21.

children   childishly

child

Name: _____   Date: _____

Spelling in Context

Use each spelling word once to complete the story.

In Someone Else's Shoes

There once lived a man named Manuel who had a wife, Alma, and four

_____. Every day Manuel went into the fields to work, like the other
<u>1</u>

_____. Alma stayed at home, like the other _____. One
<u>2</u>   <u>3</u>

day Manuel said that his work was hard, while his _____ work was easy.
                                                                              <u>4</u>

Alma looked at Manuel and said, "I wonder what would happen if husbands and

_____ traded places."
<u>5</u>

Manuel laughed and then said to Alma, "Let's trade work, and you will see how hard

a _____ life really is."
      <u>6</u>

His wife answered, "You may discover that a _____ life is not so
                                                                        <u>7</u>

easy, either." Alma hitched up the _____ and set off for the fields.
                                                         <u>8</u>

In the meantime, Manuel began to make the _____ breakfast and
                                                                      <u>9</u>

told them to brush their _____. It seemed to Manuel that as soon as he
                                        <u>10</u>

had taken care of one _____ needs, another wanted his help. He left the
                                  <u>11</u>

house and began the chores.

First he scattered grain for the _____. Then he fed the cows.
                                                  <u>12</u>

Manuel didn't feed the cats, since they were busy chasing _____. Just as
                                                                                  <u>13</u>

he began to put the _____ out to pasture, he heard the children yelling.
                              <u>14</u>

Manuel didn't know how he could watch both the children and the sheep, so he carried

the sheep up to the grass roof to graze. He tied ropes around their legs and dropped the

ropes down the chimney. He rushed to the kitchen and tied a rope around each of his

legs so that the sheep could not run away. Then Manuel went back to work. He washed

the dishes, forks, and _____. He had begun to put them on the
                                    <u>15</u>

kitchen _____ when the sheep fell off the roof. Manuel went
              <u>16</u>

_____-first up the chimney!
<u>17</u>

Out in the fields, Alma stopped working. She looked up at the sky and noticed a large _____ dark color. Alma knew

18

that it was going to rain. Many of the men were already heading home. Judging that her wagon was as full as the

_____ wagons,

19

she went home, too.

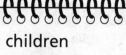

When she opened the door, Alma saw Manuel hanging upside down in the fireplace and the children running wildly about. Quickly she grabbed a knife and cut the rope.

"Well," she asked, "how do you like _____

20

work?"

Manuel never said a word about women's work again.

children
men
shelves
man's
cloud's
women
feet
woman's
women's
child's
teeth
children's
sheep
oxen
mice
geese
wife's
knives
wives
men's

★ Challenge Yourself ★

Challenge Words

larvae
thieves
mongoose's
patios

Write the Challenge Word for each clue. Check a dictionary to see if you are right. Then use separate paper to write sentences showing that you understand the meaning of each Challenge Word.

21. They take things that don't belong to them.

_____

22. These are places outside where you can relax. _____

23. This means "belonging to a kind of mammal that kills snakes."

_____

24. These will soon change into something very different. _____

Lesson 26

Words with /ûr/ or /îr/

circus

1. /ûr/ Words

_____
_____
_____
_____
_____
_____
_____
_____
_____

2. /îr/ Words

_____
_____
_____
_____
_____
_____

curve
hear
clear
learn
third
dear
circus
skirt
heard
squirt
early
birth
germ
world
cheer
period
here
circle
earn
dirty

Say and Listen

The spelling words for this lesson contain the /ûr/ or /îr/ sounds that you hear in *curve* and *hear.* Say the spelling words. Listen for the /ûr/ and /îr/ sounds.

Think and Sort

Look at the letters in each word. Think about how the /ûr/ or /îr/ sounds are spelled. Spell each word aloud.

How many spelling patterns for /ûr/ and /îr/ do you see?

1. Write the fourteen spelling words that have the /ûr/ sound. Circle the letters that spell /ûr/ in each word.

2. Write the six spelling words that have the /îr/ sound. Circle the letters that spell /îr/ in each word.

Use the steps on page 4 to study words that are hard for you.

Spelling Patterns

/ûr/	/îr/
c**ur**ve sk**ir**t l**ear**n	h**ear** p**er**iod
w**or**ld g**er**m	h**ere** ch**eer**

Name: _____   Date: _____

Spelling and Meaning

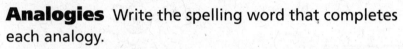

Synonyms Write the spelling word that is a synonym for each word.

1. bend   _____
2. plain   _____
3. yell   _____
4. soiled   _____

Analogies Write the spelling word that completes each analogy.

5. *Continent* is to _____ as *county* is to *state*.

6. *Ending* is to *death* as *beginning* is to _____.

7. *Too* is to *two* as *deer* is to _____.

8. *Now* is to *then* as _____ is to *there*.

9. *Listened* is to _____ as *story* is to *tale*.

10. *Spend* is to _____ as *give* is to *get*.

11. *Speak* is to *mouth* as _____ is to *ear*.

12. *Door* is to *rectangle* as *plate* is to _____.

13. *Ask* is to *question mark* as *tell* is to _____.

14. *Two* is to *second* as *three* is to _____.

15. *Pour* is to *milk* as _____ is to *toothpaste*.

16. *Blouse* is to *top* as _____ is to *bottom*.

17. *School* is to _____ as *office* is to *work*.

18. *Sad* is to *happy* as *late* is to _____.

19. *Microscope* is to _____ as *telescope* is to *star*.

Word Story   One spelling word comes from the Greek word for *circle*, *kirkos*. The spelling word names a kind of entertainment that is presented inside circular rings. Write the word.

20. _____

Family Tree: *cheer* Think about how the *cheer* words are alike in spelling and meaning. Then add another *cheer* word to the tree.

cheerfully

21. _____

cheerful   cheery

cheer

Name: _____   Date: _____

Spelling in Context

Use each spelling word once to complete the selection.

The Circus, Past and Present

People clap and _____ 1. Elephants parade and bow. Clowns _____ 2 water in each other's face. A woman in a shiny satin _____ 3 rides on a galloping white horse. You can _____ 4 lively music played on an organ and steam whistles. Where are you? You are at the _____ 5!

The circus as we know it began in England more than 200 years ago. A man named Philip Astley started performing riding tricks. He stood on his horse's back as the horse trotted in a _____ 6. This was the first circus ring. Astley's act was exciting, but one thing soon became _____ 7 to him. He needed more acts. He added acrobats, a clown, and a band. The crowd loved the show, and the circus was born!

The _____ 8 of the circus was also the beginning of many circus traditions. One tradition is that the acts are performed in a ring. Most _____ 9 circuses had only one or two rings. After a _____ 10 of time, circuses grew larger. They added a _____ 11 ring and more acts.

At the first circuses, clowns kept people laughing. Early clowns wore dressy clothes. Some later clowns dressed in wild outfits with bright colors. Others dressed in _____ 12 rags to look like "tramps."

Being in a circus is a way of life. Modern circus people travel _____ 13 and there all over the countryside. They work together like members of a large family. The

adults help children _____ to juggle, to ride, and to
                              14
care for the animals. Animals that are poorly fed do not perform well.
Neither do animals that get sick from a harmful

_____ in a dirty stall.
        15

    Many circus children grow up and _____ their
                                              16
living by doing the same act their parents did. You may have

_____ of circus families who have performed the
        17
same act for years and years. Horses and trick riders are as important
in today's circus as they were in Astley's show. It takes skill to stay on a
galloping horse when it turns a sharp _____!
                                              18

    Adults and children now enjoy the circus in countries all around

the _____. Going to the circus is a childhood
        19
memory many adults hold _____. They want their
                                  20
children to enjoy the same happy experience.

curve
hear
clear
learn
third
dear
circus
skirt
heard
squirt
early
birth
germ
world
cheer
period
here
circle
earn
dirty

★ Challenge Yourself ★

Challenge Words

courtesy
convert
worthwhile
interior

Use a dictionary to answer these questions. Then use separate paper to write sentences showing that you understand the meaning of each Challenge Word.

21. Should you go outside to see the **interior** of a
    building? _____

22. When you thank someone for a gift, are you showing **courtesy**?
    _____

23. Can you **convert** a piece of rock into gold? _____

24. If you went to a store but found that it was closed, was the trip
    worthwhile? _____

Lesson 27
Words with /ə/

automobile

1. Words with One /ə/

_____
_____
_____
_____
_____
_____
_____
_____
_____
_____

2. Words with More than One /ə/

_____
_____
_____
_____
_____
_____

together
animal
blizzard
simple
wrinkle
United States
  of America
calendar
special
winter
summer
automobile
dinosaur
Canada
address
chapter
whether
whistle
purple
tickle
wander

Say and Listen
Say the spelling words. Listen for the syllables that are not stressed.

Think and Sort
Most unstressed syllables have a weak vowel sound called **schwa**. It is shown as /ə/. Some words have one /ə/, and others have more than one.

Look at the letters in each word as you say each word again. Think about how /ə/ is spelled. Spell each word aloud. How many spelling patterns for /ə/ do you see?

1. Write the fourteen spelling words that have one /ə/ sound. Underline the letter that spells /ə/.

2. Write the six spelling words that have more than one /ə/ sound. Underline the letters that spell /ə/.

Use the steps on page 4 to study words that are hard for you.

Spelling Patterns

a	e	i	o
address	summ**e**r	an**i**mal	din**o**saur

Spelling and Meaning

Classifying Write the spelling word that belongs in each group.

1. red, blue, _____

2. hurricane, tornado, _____

3. easy, plain, _____

4. crease, crumple, _____

5. name, _____, telephone number

6. roam, stray, _____

7. train, plane, _____

8. beast, creature, _____

Definitions Write the spelling word for each definition.
Use a dictionary if you need to.

9. at the same time   _____

10. if   _____

11. North American country containing fifty states   _____

12. a main division of a book   _____

13. the season between fall and spring   _____

14. northernmost North American country   _____

15. chart showing time by days, weeks, and months _____

16. not usual   _____

17. the season between spring and fall   _____

18. to touch lightly   _____

19. to make a sound by forcing air through lips   _____

Word Story   One spelling word comes from two Greek words, *deinos* and *saurus*. *Deinos* meant "terrible" and *saurus* meant "lizard." Write the word.

20. _____

Family Tree: *simple*   Think about how the *simple* words are alike in spelling and meaning. Then add another *simple* word to the tree.

simplified

21. _____

simpler   simplify

simple

Spelling in Context

Use each spelling word once to complete the story.

An Unforgettable Day

July 7 is a day I'll never forget. I don't know _____ to look back at
1
that day as a _____ family memory or as a strange _____
2   3
in a mystery novel.

I woke up that morning with a feeling like someone was about to
_____ my stomach. I was super excited! I looked at the
4
_____ on my desk to make sure it was really the day.
5
My family was going to head out for our _____ vacation. We would
6
be leaving our house in Smallville, New York, a very small town in the
_____ and driving to a cabin just outside the mountains in
7
_____. I had never been out of the country before and was looking
8
forward to a relaxing getaway _____ with my family.
9

I looked at the clock and realized it was time to round everyone up. I grabbed a
_____ from my backpack and walked down the hallway, blowing it as
10
loudly as possible. Everyone scrambled out of their rooms, including my toddler sister and
her stuffed _____ Dino. She never went anywhere without that silly
11
_____.
12

"It's time to get ready," I yelled out. "We have one hour before it's time to leave!"
Everyone moved around like clockwork, getting dressed and doing
_____ last-minute packing. When one hour had passed, my father told
13
everyone to head downstairs to leave.

As I walked off the last step, I decided to _____ to the kitchen to
14
make sure my mom had grabbed the _____ of the cabin on the
15
refrigerator. The last thing I wanted was to drive all that way and not know where
we were going.

When I walked out the front door, I looked at my father. I noticed there was a _____ on his forehead, and his

16

nose had turned the color _____. I looked toward

17

the driveway and saw that snow had covered our

_____. A _____ had blown through

18   19

overnight, and white snow was piled high.

    "Looks like we had a _____ storm in the

20

middle of July," my father said. "I guess we're not going anywhere

today."

    So, instead of
spending the day driving
to the cabin, we played
in the snow and had a
great time. It wasn't how
I imagined our summer
vacation to begin, but it
was definitely an
unforgettable day.

Word list:

together
animal
blizzard
simple
wrinkle
United States
  of America
calendar
special
winter
summer
automobile
dinosaur
Canada
address
chapter
whether
whistle
purple
tickle
wander

★ Challenge Yourself ★

Challenge Words

burglar	missile
binoculars	dwindle

Write the Challenge Word for each clue. Check a dictionary to see if you are right. Then use separate paper to write sentences showing that you understand the meaning of each Challenge Word.

21. Things look closer when you look through these. _____
22. This can be fired at a target that is far away. _____
23. This is someone who breaks into a house to steal something. _____
24. The library's supply of books will do this if everyone checks out books.

_____

Lesson 28

Compound Words

basketball

1. _____
2. _____
3. _____
4. _____
5. _____
6. _____
7. _____
8. _____
9. _____
10. _____
11. _____
12. _____
13. _____
14. _____
15. _____
16. _____
17. _____
18. _____
19. _____
20. _____

basketball
cheeseburger
countdown
newspaper
drugstore
outside
everybody
birthday
upstairs
inside
nightmare
afternoon
anything
forever
sometimes
weekend
downtown
without
everywhere
railroad

Say and Listen

Say each spelling word. Listen for the two shorter words in each word.

Think and Sort

All of the spelling words are compound words. In a **compound word**, two words are joined to form a new word. For example, *basket + ball = basketball*. Write the spelling word that is formed from each word pair below.

1. after + noon
2. any + thing
3. for + ever
4. some + times
5. with + out
6. every + body
7. basket + ball
8. count + down
9. in + side
10. out + side
11. night + mare
12. news + paper
13. up + stairs
14. drug + store
15. every + where
16. rail + road
17. week + end
18. birth + day
19. down + town
20. cheese + burger

Use the steps on page 4 to study words that are hard for you.

Spelling Patterns

basket|ball | every|body | down|town | for|ever

Spelling and Meaning

Antonyms Complete each sentence by writing the spelling word that is an antonym of the underlined word.

1. The museum is <u>uptown</u>, but the library is _____.
2. John likes eggs <u>with</u> salt but _____ pepper.
3. I went <u>downstairs</u> as Maria went _____.
4. Customers are _____, but a clerk is <u>nowhere</u> to be found.
5. We couldn't play <u>outside</u>, so we went _____.

Compound Words Write the spelling word that can be formed by combining two words in each sentence.

6. Have you ever wished for a puppy? _____
7. The count began with ten and went down to zero. _____
8. We shop some of the times that we get together. _____
9. His birth occurred on the last day of June. _____
10. Our collie snatched the ball from the basket. _____
11. Selma wanted cheese on her burger. _____
12. Jill ran out and played on her side of the fence. _____
13. We looked at every part of the frog's body. _____
14. This unusual thing didn't come with any directions. _____
15. A rail fell off the fence and onto the road. _____
16. The pet store sells a special drug to kill fleas. _____
17. Most of the news in our paper is interesting. _____
18. We eat lunch after the clock chimes at noon. _____
19. The end of the week will be here soon. _____

Word Story   One of the spelling words was once used to name an evil spirit that sat on the chest of a sleeper. The modern meaning of the word is "a frightening dream." Write the spelling word.

20. _____

Family Tree: *countdown*   Think about how the *count* words are alike in spelling and meaning. Then add another *count* word to the tree.

countdown

21. _____

counted   uncounted

count

Spelling in Context

Use each spelling word once to complete the story.

The Best Weekend of My Life

It was Sunday, April 7, 1978. I remember the date because my tenth

_____ was the day before. I was sitting around, not doing much of
        1

_____, when my brother, Gus, walked into the room.
        2

"How would you like to take a ride into Boston with me?" he asked. He pulled out

two tickets to the Celtics _____ game. "Happy birthday!"
                                    3

"I can't believe it!" I screamed. "How did you get those tickets?

_____ in Boston wants to see John Havlicek's last game!"
        4

He smiled. "Well, I'd like to say I got them _____ any trouble, but I
                                                      5

cannot tell a lie. Waiting _____ the ticket office at the Garden was a real
                                6

_____. The crowds were unbelievable!"
        7

I ran _____ to get my jacket and raced to the
              8

_____ station with Gus. We caught the train that went into
        9

_____ Boston and arrived a little after
        10

noon. All the stores in the train station and even the little

_____ were filled with Havlicek buttons. I
        11

didn't care much about eating anything, but Gus bought us

each a big _____, and then we went
                  12

_____.
        13

The Garden was packed with screaming fans. The

crowd was so loud that _____ I couldn't
                                14

even hear Gus. Banners hung _____. Some
                                      15

said, "Boston loves Hondo." That was Havlicek's nickname.

When the speeches were over, Hondo stepped up to the microphone and said, "Thank you, Boston. I love you!" The fans went wild. It seemed as though they cheered _____.
16

      Then the game began. Hondo scored 29 points. A few minutes before the game ended, he was pulled, and the crowd stood up. It was the end of a 16-year career. In the last seconds of the game, the fans began the _____. The Celtics won, but it was John
17
Havlicek's day. An article in the _____ reported that he
18
turned the lights out in the Garden that night.

      Years have passed since then, but those two days stand out in my memory. My tenth birthday on Saturday and the Havlicek game on Sunday _____ made those two days the best
19
_____ of my life.
20

basketball	
cheeseburger	
countdown	
newspaper	
drugstore	
outside	
everybody	
birthday	
upstairs	
inside	
nightmare	
afternoon	
anything	
forever	
sometimes	
weekend	
downtown	
without	
everywhere	
railroad	

★ Challenge Yourself ★

Challenge Words

farmland

dewdrops

crossroads

dishwasher

What do you think each Challenge Word means? Check a dictionary to see if you are right. Then use separate paper to write sentences showing that you understand the meaning of each Challenge Word.

21. He loaded the dirty plates and cups into the **dishwasher**.

22. This morning the **dewdrops** on the grass tickled my bare feet.

23. To make driving safer, city workers placed stop signs at the **crossroads**.

24. Farmland must have good soil for raising crops.

© Harcourt Achieve Inc. All rights reserved.

Lesson 29

Abbreviations

1 gal

1. Street Addresses

_____
_____
_____
_____
_____

2. Units of Measurement

_____
_____
_____
_____
_____
_____
_____
_____
_____
_____
_____
_____

3. Temperature Scales

_____
_____

Ave.
qt
Rd.
cm
F
in
St.
ft
Hwy.
gal
yd
km
l
mi
c
Blvd.
pt
C
m
Rte.

Say and Listen
Say the spelling word that each abbreviation stands for.

Think and Sort
All of the spelling words are abbreviations. An **abbreviation** is a shortened version of a word. Abbreviations used in street addresses end with a period. Abbreviations of units of measurement and temperature scales do not.

1. Write the six abbreviations used in street addresses.

2. Write the twelve abbreviations for units of measurement.

3. Write the two abbreviations for temperature scales.

• Use the steps on page 4 to study words that are hard for you. •

Spelling Patterns

Addresses	Units of Measurement	Temperature Scales
Rte.	qt	C
St.	km	F

© Harcourt Achieve Inc. All rights reserved.
Core Skills Spelling 4, SV 9781419034084

Spelling and Meaning

Trading Places Write the abbreviation that can be used instead of the word.

1. Fahrenheit _____
2. gallon _____
3. cup _____
4. yard _____
5. centimeter _____
6. quart _____
7. liter _____
8. Celsius _____
9. pint _____
10. mile _____
11. inch _____
12. kilometer _____
13. foot _____

Clues Write the spelling word for each underlined word.

14. 315 Rose Boulevard _____
15. Route 2, Box 56 _____
16. Box 1010, Highway 47 _____
17. 224 Main Street _____
18. 2067 Green Road _____
19. 1007 Bright Avenue _____

Word Story   One spelling word comes from the Greek word *metron*, which meant "a measure or a rule." The spelling word is an abbreviation that means "39.37 inches." Write the abbreviation.

20. _____

Family Tree: *quart* The abbreviation *qt* stands for *quart*. Think about how the *quart* words are alike in spelling and meaning. Then add another *quart* word to the tree.

quarterly

21. _____

quartet   quarts

quart

www.harcourtschoolsupply.com
© Harcourt Achieve Inc. All rights reserved.

Lesson 29: Abbreviations
Core Skills Spelling 4, SV 9781419034084

Spelling in Context

Use each abbreviation once to complete the selection.

Dear Ming and Lan,

Please make Quick Wheatloaf tonight. You'll need to go to Super Mart and pick up the ingredients. Super Mart is only 5 _____ from our house. (Lan, is this distance equal to 7 or 8 _____? I think you will know the answer, since you just made an A on your measurement test!) Here are a map and the directions.

North on _____ 25, right onto Lansing _____,
right onto Circle _____, left on Lakes _____,
right on Oak _____. Store will be on your left.
If you reach the freeway, _____ 12, you've gone too far. You may want to park in the east lot because it's shady. The east lot is where they had the hundred-_____ dash for free groceries last year.

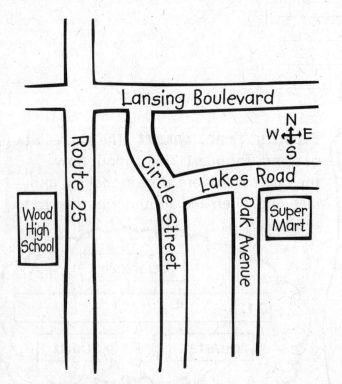

Raisins are on a high shelf in the store. Ming, you'll need to get the raisins, since you are at least five _____ six _____ tall. Lan can gather the other ingredients.

Love, Mom

P.S. Lan, don't forget to pick up a _____ of ribbon and a _____ ruler for your math project.

Quick Wheatloaf Recipe

Ingredients

1¾ cups whole wheat flour   ½ cup molasses

2 tablespoons wheat germ   ½ pint buttermilk or yogurt

½ teaspoon baking soda   ½ cup raisins

pinch of salt

      Mix 1¾ cups flour with wheat germ, baking soda, and salt.
Add ½ _____ molasses and ½ _____
         14   **15**
buttermilk to dry ingredients. Stir in raisins. Put dough into
greased loaf pan and bake at 375° _____ or
                                         16
190° _____ for 30 minutes.
         17

      Serving Suggestions   For 4 people, serve Quick Wheatloaf
with a _____ of orange juice or milk. This equals
             18
a little more than 1 _____. For more than 4
                      19
people, serve bread with a _____ of apple cider.
                         20

Ave.
qt
Rd.
cm
F
in
St.
ft
Hwy.
gal
yd
km
l
mi
c
Blvd.
pt
C
m
Rte.

★ Challenge Yourself ★

Challenge Words

oz	lb
g	kg

Write the Challenge Word for each clue. Check a
dictionary to see if you are right. Then use separate
paper to write sentences showing that you understand
the meaning of each Challenge Word.

21. My name means one thousand grams. _____

22. I am much less than an ounce. I am used by scientists. _____

23. Most people in the United States use me to tell how much
they weigh. _____

24. I am about the same as 28 grams. _____

© Harcourt Achieve Inc. All rights reserved.
Core Skills Spelling 4, SV 9781419034084

Lesson 30

Words About the Universe

Saturn

Say and Listen
Say each spelling word. Listen for the number of syllables in each word.

Think and Sort
All of the spelling words are terms that people use to write about the universe.

1. Write the one spelling word that contains two words. Divide each word into syllables.

2. Write the two spelling words that have one syllable.

3. Write the eight spelling words that have two syllables.

4. Write the eight spelling words that have three syllables.

5. Write the one spelling word that has four syllables.

Word List:
rotate
gravity
Jupiter
Pluto
solar system
galaxy
Saturn
universe
Venus
meteor
Earth
satellite
Neptune
comet
Uranus
revolve
Mercury
constellation
Mars
planets

1. Two Words
_____

2. One-Syllable Words
_____
_____

3. Two-Syllable Words
_____
_____
_____
_____
_____
_____
_____
_____

4. Three-Syllable Words
_____
_____
_____
_____
_____
_____
_____
_____

5. Four-Syllable Word
_____

• • • • • •
Use the steps
on page 4 to
study words
that are hard
for you.
• • • • • •

Spelling Patterns

One Syllable	Two Syllables
Mars	Sat•urn

Three Syllables	Four Syllables
Ju•pi•ter	con•stel•la•tion

www.harcourtschoolsupply.com
© Harcourt Achieve Inc. All rights reserved.

Lesson 30: Words About the Universe
Core Skills Spelling 4, SV 9781419034084

Spelling and Meaning

Clues Write the spelling word for each clue.

1. planet closest to the sun   _____
2. seventh planet from the sun   _____
3. fourth planet; the "red" one   _____
4. eighth planet; named for the Roman sea god   _____
5. only planet that can support animal life   _____
6. second planet; named for a Roman goddess   _____
7. the planet with "rings"   _____
8. the "dwarf planet"   _____
9. fifth planet from the sun; the largest planet   _____

What's the Answer? Write a spelling word that answers each question.

10. What moves around the sun and has a long tail?   _____
11. What falls through space toward Earth?   _____
12. What word refers to everything in space?   _____
13. What names a communications object that circles Earth? _____
14. The Big Dipper is an example of what?   _____
15. Mars, Jupiter, and Venus are examples of what?   _____
16. What do planets do as they travel around the sun?   _____
17. What keeps us from falling off Earth?   _____
18. What does Earth do as it spins on its axis?   _____
19. What are the sun and all the planets called as a group? _____

Word **Story** One spelling word means "a large collection of stars." It comes from *galaxias*, a Greek word meaning "milky." Write the spelling word.

20. _____

Family Tree: *revolve* Think about how the *revolve* words are alike in spelling and meaning. Then add another *revolve* word to the tree.

revolution

21. _____

revolves   revolved

revolve

Spelling in Context

Use each spelling word once to complete the selection.

The Universe

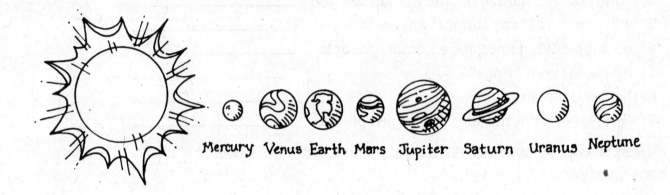

Mercury Venus Earth Mars Jupiter Saturn Uranus Neptune

Earth is just one tiny part of the great _____. All around us in space
lie millions of other _____ and stars. We are part of a
_____, or family of stars, called the Milky Way. Our sun is only one of
the stars that make up the Milky Way.

The sun and all of the things that move around it in space are called the
_____. The sun has enough _____, or pull, to keep our
solar system in order. Nine planets _____ around the sun. As they move,
the planets also spin around, or _____. Some planets have natural objects
that revolve around them! These objects are called moons, or satellites. Earth has only one
_____, while Jupiter has 16! The 4 planets nearest the sun are
_____, _____, _____, and
_____. These planets are made mostly of iron and rock. The next 4
planets are _____, _____; _____, and
_____. They seem to be made up chiefly of gases. _____
was once considered to be the farthest planet from the sun. In 2006, however, scientists
decided it didn't meet the new definition of a planet. Now it is classified as a "dwarf
planet."

There are many other interesting parts of the universe. Star watchers like to pick out groups of stars. A large

_____ called the Big Dipper is a favorite. Others
18

enjoy spotting a shooting star, or _____, blazing
19

through the sky. Some people study the bright tail of a

_____.
20

The universe holds many secrets. As we send off each new space probe, we come a little closer to understanding what lies out there in space.

rotate
gravity
Jupiter
Pluto
solar system
galaxy
Saturn
universe
Venus
meteor
Earth
satellite
Neptune
comet
Uranus
revolve
Mercury
constellation
Mars
planets

★ Challenge Yourself ★

Challenge Words

physics

vastness

takeoff

technology

Use a dictionary to answer these questions. Then use separate paper to write sentences showing that you understand the meaning of each Challenge Word.

21. Is it important to understand **physics** before you start to build a spaceship? _____

22. Can we explore the **vastness** of outer space in one day? _____

23. If a rocket is ready for **takeoff**, is it ready to land? _____

24. Without **technology**, could people walk on the moon? _____

Answer Key

Page 6
1. past, match, ask, snack, stamp, magic, pass, happen, answer, travel, plastic, grass, began, crack, glad, branch, half, banana
2. laugh, aunt

Page 7
1. crack
2. happen
3. magic
4. travel
5. stamp
6. grass
7. plastic
8. began
9. glad
10. half
11. answer
12. snack
13. banana
14. branch
15. laugh
16. aunt
17. past
18. ask
19. pass
20. match
21. Answers will vary; a suggested answer is *passing*.

Pages 8–9
1. ask
2. answer
3. banana
4. plastic
5. snack
6. past
7. began
8. pass
9. magic
10. half
11. match
12. crack
13. happen
14. travel
15. aunt
16. branch
17. grass
18. stamp
19. glad
20. laugh
21–24. Definitions and sentences will vary.

Page 10
1. awake, chase, mistake, trade, waste, taste, plane, space, state, shape
2. paid, plain, afraid, trail, wait, waist
3. eight, weight, neighbor
4. break

Page 11
1. plain
2. plane
3. waste
4. waist
5. weight
6. wait
7. taste
8. chase
9. trade
10. trail
11. state
12. space
13. paid
14. shape
15. eight
16. break
17. mistake
18. afraid
19. awake
20. neighbor
21. Answers will vary; a suggested answer is *breaking*.

Pages 12–13
1. neighbor
2. afraid
3. plain
4. space
5. mistake
6. state
7. paid
8. plane
9. trade
10. wait
11. trail
12. eight
13. break
14. chase
15. waste
16. awake
17. taste
18. shape
19. weight
20. waist
21. yes
22. no
23. no
24. yes
Sentences will vary.

Page 14
1. edge, ever, never, echo, energy, fence, stretch, yesterday, desert
2. bread, ready, heavy, health, breakfast, weather, sweater
3. again, against
4. friend
5. guess

Page 15
1. desert
2. health
3. friend
4. guess
5. heavy
6. never
7. edge
8. against
9. yesterday
10. ready
11. again
12. ever
13. weather
14. bread
15. sweater
16. fence
17. stretch
18. echo
19. energy
20. breakfast
21. Answers will vary; a suggested answer is *friendly*.

Pages 16–17
1. weather
2. sweater
3. energy
4. health
5. stretch
6. never
7. echo
8. desert
9. heavy
10. against
11. fence
12. breakfast
13. ready
14. bread
15. yesterday
16. ever
17. friend
18. again
19. edge
20. guess
21. cleanse
22. sheriff
23. deafen
24. kennel
Sentences will vary.

Page 18
1. season, scream, reason, beach, teach, means, speak, leaf, treat, peace, please
2. knee, queen, between, sweep, sweet, speech, seem, freeze, squeeze

Page 19
1. sweep
2. queen
3. leaf
4. knee
5. scream
6. between
7. sweet
8. means
9. please
10. season
11. treat
12. speak
13. seem
14. speech
15. beach
16. squeeze
17. reason
18. freeze
19. peace
20. teach
21. Answers will vary; a suggested answer is *sweetest*.

Pages 20–21
1. season
2. leaf
3. speak
4. seem
5. knee
6. speech
7. sweet
8. teach
9. means
10. reason
11. squeeze
12. freeze
13. beach
14. peace
15. please
16. scream
17. between
18. sweep
19. treat
20. queen
21. conceal
22. meek
23. treason
24. beacon
Sentences will vary.

Page 22
1. Dr.
2. March, May, June
3. Friday, Thursday, July, August, Sunday, Monday, Tuesday, Wednesday, April
4. October, December, September, November, Saturday
5. February, January

Page 23
1. February
2. Sunday
3. Tuesday
4. December
5. September
6. Saturday
7. November
8. Wednesday
9. April
10. Monday
11. October
12. Thursday
13. August
14. Dr.
15. May
16. June
17. March
18. July
19. Friday
20. January
21. Answers will vary; a suggested answer is *sunned*.

Pages 24–25
1. Sunday
2. Monday
3. Tuesday
4. Wednesday
5. Friday
6. Thursday
7. Saturday
8. January
9. February
10. March
11. April
12. May
13. June
14. July
15. August
16. September
17. October
18. November
19. December
20. Dr.
21. yes
22. no
23. governor
24. yes
Sentences will vary.

Page 26
1. zebra, secret
2. easy, every, body, family, copy, busy, city, angry, plenty, hungry, sorry
3. evening
4. people
5. radio, piano, ski, pizza
6. police

Page 27
1. radio
2. secret
3. police
4. sorry
5. busy
6. ski
7. pizza
8. zebra
9. copy
10. city
11. body
12. easy
13. every
14. angry
15. evening
16. people
17. plenty
18. family
19. hungry
20. piano
21. Answers will vary; a suggested answer is *secretly*.

Pages 28–29
1. body
2. people
3. evening
4. pizza
5. piano
6. hungry
7. easy
8. busy
9. secret
10. plenty
11. every
12. city
13. Family
14. zebra
15. copy
16. radio
17. police
18. angry
19. ski
20. sorry

Page 30
1. village
2. package
3. gym

Page 31
1. pitch
2. different
3. begin
4. quick
5. thick
6. interesting
7. written
8. deliver
9. chicken
10. inch
11. bridge
12. middle
13. picture
14. village
15. guitar
16. package
17. itch
18. building
19. gym
20. picnic
21. Answers will vary; a suggested answer is *delivered*.

Pages 32–33
1. begin
2. different
3. middle
4. building
5. chicken
6. village
7. quick
8. inch
9. thick
10. written
11. interesting
12. package
13. deliver
14. bridge
15. gym
16. pitch
17. picnic
18. guitar
19. itch
20. picture
21–24. Definitions and sentences will vary.

Page 34
1. night, mighty, fight, flight, right, might, midnight, tonight, lightning, highway, high, bright, sight
2. dry, spy, supply, reply, deny
3. tie, die

Page 35
1. bright
2. right
3. mighty
4. night
5. lightning
6. high
7. sight
8. reply
9. deny
10. dry
11. midnight
12. tie
13. might
14. flight
15. fight
16. die
17. tonight
18. supply
19. spy
20. highway
21. Answers will vary; a suggested answer is *tied*.

Pages 36–37
1. might
2. sight
3. night
4. highway
5. lightning
6. bright
7. high
8. tie
9. deny
10. flight
11. dry
12. right
13. mighty
14. supply
15. reply
16. fight
17. midnight
18. die
19. tonight
20. spy
21–24. Definitions and sentences will vary.

Page 38
1. life, knife, awhile, sunshine, smile, slide, beside, twice, write, surprise, size, wise
2. quiet, giant, climb, blind, behind, child, iron
3. buy

Page 39
1. surprise
2. giant
3. sunshine
4. behind
5. quiet
6. beside
7. iron
8. awhile
9. knife
10. smile
11. size
12. twice
13. life
14. buy
15. child
16. slide
17. climb
18. wise
19. blind
20. write
21. Answers will vary; a suggested answer is *quietly*.

Pages 40–41
1. life
2. slide
3. iron
4. behind
5. child
6. sunshine
7. blind
8. smile
9. surprise
10. knife
11. twice
12. size
13. giant
14. beside
15. buy
16. quiet
17. awhile
18. climb
19. wise
20. write
21–24. Definitions and sentences will vary.

Page 42
1. brothers, trees, pockets, rocks, hikes, gloves
2. dishes, classes, buses, brushes, inches, branches, peaches, foxes, boxes
3. families, pennies, cities, babies, stories

Page 43
1. buses
2. cities
3. rocks
4. brothers
5. pennies
6. boxes
7. inches
8. foxes
9. branches
10. babies
11. stories
12. families
13. trees
14. pockets
15. hikes
16. gloves
17. dishes
18. classes
19. brushes
20. peaches
21. Answers will vary; a suggested answer is *classifying*.

Pages 44–45
1. classes
2. brothers
3. cities
4. buses
5. gloves
6. branches
7. brushes
8. foxes
9. families
10. babies
11. stories
12. hikes
13. boxes
14. peaches
15. dishes
16. trees
17. rocks
18. inches
19. pockets
20. pennies
21–24. Definitions and sentences will vary.

www.harcourtschoolsupply.com
© Harcourt Achieve Inc. All rights reserved.

Answer Key
Core Skills Spelling 4, SV 9781419034084

Page 46
1. hobby, model, forgot, doctor, contest, object, o'clock, cotton, dollar, solve, knock, problem, bottom, beyond, knot, hospital
2. wash, wallet, watch, swallow

Page 47
1. swallow
2. knock
3. wash
4. watch
5. dollar
6. solve
7. cotton
8. contest
9. object
10. wallet
11. model
12. beyond
13. doctor
14. forgot
15. o'clock
16. knot
17. bottom
18. hobby
19. problem
20. hospital
21. Answers will vary; a suggested answer is *washes*.

Pages 48–49
1. model
2. hobby
3. wallet
4. dollar
5. contest
6. wash
7. watch
8. swallow
9. problem
10. solve
11. cotton
12. knot
13. forgot
14. bottom
15. beyond
16. knock
17. o'clock
18. hospital
19. doctor
20. object
21. yes
22. yes
23. no
24. no
Sentences will vary.

Page 50
1. clothes, total, ocean, obey, pony, poem, almost, only, comb, motor, hotel, zero, program
2. oak, throat, coach, coast, soap
3. goes, toe

Page 51
1. coast
2. almost
3. obey
4. total
5. goes
6. ocean
7. only
8. program
9. soap
10. zero
11. hotel
12. pony
13. comb
14. throat
15. poem
16. toe
17. oak
18. coach
19. clothes
20. motor
21. Answers will vary; a suggested answer is *combing*.

Pages 52–53
1. almost
2. hotel
3. soap
4. ocean
5. only
6. obey
7. coast
8. motor
9. goes
10. total
11. poem
12. clothes
13. comb
14. throat
15. zero
16. oak
17. pony
18. toe
19. program
20. coach
21. enclosure
22. host
23. foe
24. appropriate
Sentences will vary.

Page 54
1. froze, alone, broke, explode, chose, close, nose, those, stole
2. below, elbow, knows, pillow, own, hollow, shadow, slowly, tomorrow, window
3. though

Page 55
1. hollow
2. broke
3. close
4. slowly
5. froze
6. below
7. alone
8. stole
9. pillow
10. elbow
11. chose
12. tomorrow
13. nose
14. knows
15. explode
16. shadow
17. own
18. those
19. though
20. window

Pages 56–57
1. shadow
2. window
3. hollow
4. tomorrow
5. chose
6. stole
7. Slowly
8. close
9. those
10. froze
11. though
12. knows
13. elbow
14. below
15. broke
16. own
17. alone
18. explode
19. pillow
20. nose
21–24. Definitions and sentences will vary.

Page 58
1. suddenly, knuckle, brush, button, fudge, hunt, until, subject, under, jungle, hundred
2. rough, trouble, touch, couple, enough, tough, country, double
3. does

Page 59
1. brush
2. rough
3. hunt
4. fudge
5. knuckle
6. double
7. tough
8. under
9. does
10. subject
11. until
12. country
13. hundred
14. couple
15. trouble
16. touch
17. suddenly
18. enough
19. jungle
20. button
21. Answers will vary; a suggested answer is *roughest*.

Pages 60–61
1. until
2. enough
3. hunt
4. subject
5. Does
6. rough
7. brush
8. knuckle
9. country
10. double
11. button
12. fudge
13. couple
14. under
15. trouble
16. Suddenly
17. touch
18. hundred
19. jungle
20. tough
21. no
22. yes
23. no
24. yes
Sentences will vary.

Page 62
1. weren't, doesn't, isn't, wouldn't, wasn't, aren't, don't, hadn't, haven't, didn't, shouldn't, couldn't
2. a. I'm, b. that's, c. we're, d. let's, e. they've, f. you'd, g. she'd, h. they'll

Page 63
1. I'm
2. they've
3. she'd
4. we're
5. you'd
6. let's
7. they'll
8. that's
9. weren't
10. didn't
11. don't
12. doesn't
13. wasn't
14. haven't
15. wouldn't
16 shouldn't
17. isn't
18. aren't
19. hadn't
20. couldn't
21. Answers will vary; a suggested answer is *he'd*.

Pages 64–65
1. isn't
2. wasn't
3. You'd
4. she'd
5. weren't
6. Let's
7. We're
8. couldn't
9. didn't
10. They'll
11. hadn't
12. wouldn't
13. aren't
14. I'm
15. doesn't
16. don't
17. They've
18. haven't
19. shouldn't
20. that's
21. There are
22. should have
23. must have
24. it would
Sentences will vary.

Page 66
1. wonderful, discover, among, front, other, brother, money, cover, month, monkey, sponge, nothing, stomach, once, another, won
2. done, above, become
3. blood

Page 67
1. above
2. front
3. done
4. won
5. wonderful
6. nothing
7. brother
8. stomach
9. once
10. become
11. blood
12. sponge
13. month
14. among
15. monkey
16. other
17. money
18. another
19. cover
20. discover
21. Answers will vary; a suggested answer is *uncovered*.

Pages 68–69
1. front
2. monkey
3. wonderful
4. blood
5. cover
6. above
7. month
8. stomach
9. brother
10. another
11. discover
12. other
13. sponge
14. won
15. among
16. once
17. money
18. done
19. become
20. nothing
21–24. Definitions and sentences will vary.

Page 70
1. wool, understood, cooked, stood, notebook, brook, wooden, good-bye
2. full, bush, sugar, pull, pudding, during
3. should, could, would, yours
4. wolf, woman

Page 71
1. pull
2. woman
3. during

Pages 72–73
1. pull
2. wool
3. would
4. bush
5. wolf
6. wooden
7. brook
8. stood
9. woman
10. should
11. could
12. understood
13. sugar
14. pudding
15. cooked
16. full
17. book
18. yours
19. during
20. good-bye
21. rural
22. swoosh
23. misunderstood
24. bookstore
Sentences will vary.

Page 74
1. goose, balloon, too, cartoon, loose, shoot, choose
2. knew, grew, new
3. truly, truth
4. cougar, route, soup, group, through
5. beautiful, two, fruit

Page 75
1. shoot
2. new
3. route
4. through
5. too
6. knew
7. two
8. beautiful
9. truth
10. group
11. balloon
12. loose
13. goose
14. fruit
15. truly
16. soup
17. cartoon
18. choose
19. grew

Pages 76–77
1. group
2. goose
3. beautiful
4. choose
5. two
6. too
7. cougar
8. loose
9. truly
10. fruit
11. route
12. knew
13. soup
14. new
15. through
16. grew
17. balloon
18. shoot
19. cartoon
20. truth
21. yes
22. no
23. yes
24. yes
Sentences will vary.

Page 78
1. loud, counter, hours, sour, cloud, ours, south, mouth, noun, proud
2. somehow, powerful, crowd, growl, towel, crowded, vowel, shower, crown, tower

Page 79
1. crown
2. hours
3. mouth
4. crowd
5. sour
6. loud
7. shower
8. growl
9. south
10. powerful
11. ours
12. crowded
13. counter
14. somehow
15. tower
16. towel
17. cloud
18. proud
19. vowel
20. noun
21. Answers will vary; a suggested answer is *powerfully*.

Pages 80–81
1. somehow
2. noun
3. crown
4. shower
5. cloud
6. mouth
7. hours
8. ours
9. vowel
10. loud
11. growl
12. south
13. proud
14. powerful
15. tower
16. counter
17. towel
18. sour
19. crowd
20. crowded
21. counselor
22. encounter
23. blouse
24. drowsy
Sentences will vary.

Page 82
1. asked, trying, carrying
2. hoping, changed, pleased, caused, traded, closing, invited, tasted, saving, writing
3. swimming, beginning, jogging
4. studied, copied, dried, cried

Page 83
1. carrying
2. swimming
3. jogging
4. tasted
5. writing
6. cried
7. studied
8. traded
9. saving
10. hoping
11. closing
12. asked
13. pleased
14. copied
15. invited
16. beginning
17. dried
18. changed
19. caused
20. trying
21. Answers will vary; a suggested answer is *unpleasant*.

Pages 84–85
1. carrying
2. swimming
3. jogging
4. asked
5. trying
6. pleased
7. studied
8. closing
9. caused
10. tasted
11. beginning
12. writing
13. changed
14. traded
15. Hoping
16. copied
17. invited
18. dried
19. cried
20. saving
21–24. Definitions and sentences will vary.

© Harcourt Achieve Inc. All rights reserved.

Page 86
1. enjoy, destroy, employ, employer, loyal, royal, voyage, loyalty, soybean
2. coin, moisture, spoil, point, poison, soil, join, avoid, voice, noise, choice

Page 87
1. voyage
2. poison
3. soil
4. loyal
5. choice
6. coin
7. point
8. voice
9. employer
10. soybean
11. loyalty
12. moisture
13. destroy
14. join
15. spoil
16. enjoy
17. noise
18. employ
19. avoid
20. royal
21. Answers will vary; a suggested answer is *pointing*.

Pages 88–89
1. voyage
2. loyal
3. loyalty
4. employer
5. voice
6. noise
7. coin
8. soybean
9. royal
10. point
11. choice
12. moisture
13. soil
14. destroy
15. avoid
16. poison
17. employ
18. enjoy
19. join
20. spoil
21. poise
22. toil
23. pointless
24. appoint
Sentences will vary.

Page 90
1. pause, cause, because, author, applaud, autumn
2. strong, wrong, coffee, gone, offer, often, office
3. taught, caught, daughter
4. brought, bought, thought
5. already

Page 91
1. taught

2. applaud
3. strong
4. wrong
5. bought
6. thought
7. autumn
8. caught
9. author
10. pause
11. daughter
12. brought
13. offer
14. often
15. gone
16. already
17. office
18. because
19. cause
20. coffee
21. Answers will vary; a suggested answer is *thoughtfully*.

Pages 92–93
1. daughter
2. already
3. taught
4. author
5. office
6. coffee
7. bought
8. autumn
9. applaud
10. strong
11. thought
12. wrong
13. because
14. brought
15. offer
16. caught
17. cause
18. pause
19. gone
20. often
21. no
22. yes
23. yes
24. no
Sentences will vary.

Page 94
1. lawn, straw, dawn, crawl, yawn
2. toward, water, quart, warm
3. morning, score, north, explore, before, shore, chorus, important, orbit, report, popcorn

Page 95
1. popcorn
2. lawn
3. straw
4. important
5. toward
6. yawn
7. orbit
8. score
9. report
10. dawn
11. morning
12. before
13. north
14. chorus
15. explore
16. crawl
17. warm
18. quart

19. water
20. shore
21. Answers will vary; a suggested answer is *exploration*.

Pages 96–97
1. morning
2. warm
3. orbit
4. popcorn
5. toward
6. quart
7. water
8. dawn
9. crawl
10. yawn
11. explore
12. important
13. shore
14. north
15. lawn
16. Straw
17. chorus
18. report
19. before
20. score
21–24. Definitions and sentences will vary.

Page 98
1. sharp, marbles, smart, large, heart, scarf, apart, alarm
2. share, they're, their, where, careful, square, there, stairs, fair, air, fare, stares
21. Answers will vary; a suggested answer is *childhood*.

Page 99
1. air
2. sharp
3. alarm
4. scarf
5. smart
6. large
7. apart
8. careful
9. square
10. share
11. marbles
12. where
13. their
14. fair
15. stairs
16. fare
17. there
18. they're
19. stares
20. heart
21. Answers will vary; a suggested answer is *fairness*.

Pages 100–101
1. alarm
2. marbles
3. scarf
4. stairs
5. smart
6. careful
7. square
8. air
9. heart
10. large
11. Their
12. stares
13. there
14. They're
15. sharp

16. apart
17. share
18. Where
19. fair
20. fare
21–24. Definitions and sentences will vary.

Page 102
1. children, men, shelves, women, feet, teeth, sheep, oxen, mice, geese, knives, wives
2. man's, cloud's, woman's, women's, child's, children's, wife's, men's

Page 103
1. mice
2. shelves
3. geese
4. sheep
5. knives
6. feet
7. teeth
8. men
9. oxen
10. women
11. children
12. man's
13. child's
14. wife's
15. cloud's
16. women's
17. children's
18. men's
19. woman's
20. wives
21. Answers will vary; a suggested answer is *cheered*.

Pages 104–105
1. children
2. men
3. women
4. wife's
5. wives
6. man's
7. woman's
8. oxen
9. children's
10. teeth
11. child's
12. geese
13. mice
14. sheep
15. knives
16. shelves
17. feet
18. cloud's
19. men's
20. women's
21. thieves
22. patios
23. mongoose's
24. larvae
Sentences will vary.

Page 106
1. curve, learn, third, circus, skirt, heard, squirt, early, birth, germ, world, circle, earn, dirty
2. hear, clear, dear, cheer,

period, here

Page 107
1. curve
2. clear
3. cheer
4. dirty
5. world
6. birth
7. dear
8. here
9. heard
10. earn
11. hear
12. circle
13. period
14. third
15. squirt
16. skirt
17. learn
18. early
19. germ
20. circus
21. Answers will vary; a suggested answer is *simplest*.

Pages 108–109
1. cheer
2. squirt
3. skirt
4. hear
5. circus
6. circle
7. clear
8. birth
9. early
10. period
11. third
12. dirty
13. here
14. learn
15. germ
16. earn
17. heard
18. curve
19. world
20. dear
21. no
22. yes
23. no
24. no
Sentences will vary.

Page 110
1. blizzard, simple, wrinkle, special, winter, summer, dinosaur, address, chapter, whether, whistle, purple, tickle, wander
2. together, animal, United States of America, calendar, automobile, Canada

Page 111
1. purple
2. blizzard
3. simple
4. wrinkle
5. address
6. wander
7. automobile
8. animal
9. together
10. whether
11. United States of America
12. chapter

13. winter
14. Canada
15. calendar
16. special
17. summer
18. tickle
19. whistle
20. dinosaur
21. Answers will vary; a suggested answer is *counting*.

Pages 112–113
1. whether
2. special
3. chapter
4. tickle
5. calendar
6. summer
7. United States of America
8. Canada
9. together
10. whistle
11. animal/ dinosaur
12. dinosaur/ animal
13. simple
14. wander
15. address
16. wrinkle
17. purple
18. automobile
19. blizzard
20. winter
21. binoculars
22. missile
23. burglar
24. dwindle
Sentences will vary.

Page 114
1. afternoon
2. anything
3. forever
4. sometimes
5. without
6. everybody
7. basketball
8. countdown
9. inside
10. outside
11. nightmare
12. newspaper
13. upstairs
14. drugstore
15. everywhere
16. railroad
17. weekend
18. birthday
19. downtown
20. cheeseburger

Page 115
1. downtown
2. without
3. upstairs
4. everywhere
5. inside
6. forever
7. countdown
8. sometimes
9. birthday
10. basketball
11. cheeseburger
12. outside
13. everybody
14. anything
15. railroad
16. drugstore

17. newspaper
18. afternoon
19. weekend
20. nightmare
21. Answers will vary; a suggested answer is *counting*.

Pages 116–117
1. birthday
2. anything
3. basketball
4. Everybody
5. without
6. outside
7. nightmare
8. upstairs
9. railroad
10. downtown
11. drugstore
12. cheeseburger
13. inside
14. sometimes
15. everywhere
16. forever
17. countdown
18. newspaper
19. afternoon
20. weekend
21–24. Definitions and sentences will vary.

Page 118
1. Ave., Rd., St., Hwy., Blvd., Rte.,
2. qt, cm, in, ft, gal, yd, km, l, mi, c, pt, m
3. F, C

Page 119
1. F
2. gal
3. c
4. yd
5. cm
6. qt
7. l
8. C
9. pt
10. mi
11. in
12. km
13. ft
14. Blvd.
15. Rte.
16. Hwy.
17. St.
18. Rd.
19. Ave.
20. m
21. Answers will vary; a suggested answer is *quarter*.

Pages 120–121
1. mi
2. km
3. Rte.
4. Blvd.
5. St.
6. Rd.
7. Ave.
8. Hwy.
9. yd
10. ft
11. in
12. m
13. cm
14. c
15. pt
16. F

17. C
18. qt
19. l
20. gal
21. kg
22. g
23. lb
24. oz
Sentences will vary.

Page 122
1. so-lar system
2. Earth, Mars
3. rotate, Pluto, Saturn, Venus, Neptune, comet, revolve, planets
4. gravity, Jupiter, galaxy, universe, meteor, satellite, Uranus, Mercury
5. constellation

Page 123
1. Mercury
2. Uranus
3. Mars
4. Neptune
5. Earth
6. Venus
7. Saturn
8. Pluto
9. Jupiter
10. comet
11. meteor
12. universe
13. satellite
14. constellation
15. planets
16. revolve
17. gravity
18. rotate
19. solar system
20. galaxy
21. Answers will vary; a suggested answer is *revolving*.

Pages 124–125
1. universe
2. planets
3. galaxy
4. solar system
5. gravity
6. revolve
7. rotate
8. satellite
9. Mercury
10. Venus
11. Earth
12. Mars
13. Jupiter
14. Saturn
15. Uranus
16. Neptune
17. Pluto
18. constellation
19. meteor
20. comet
21. yes
22. no
23. no
24. no
Sentences will vary.

www.harcourtschoolsupply.com
© Harcourt Achieve Inc. All rights reserved.

Answer Key
Core Skills Spelling 4, SV 9781419034084